Best wishes!

7/17/97

For any executive, this book is a must. Writing in elegant simplicity, Guy Hale manages to capture what helps leaders succeed.

John J. Fischer, *President and CEO,* Akashic Memories Corporation

Terrific toolkit. Should be required reading for any company setting up operations in China or India.

Mike DeNoma, *CEO,* Asia Foods, Hong Kong

As knowledge is becoming more and more critical as a source of competitive advantage, so high-quality analytical skills are essential. In its systematic approach to the key elements of thinking—situation appraisal, analyzing problems, making decisions, analyzing plans and being innovative—*The Leader's Edge* is an invaluable guide. Read it and maintain your competitive edge!

Peter Sheldrake, *Executive Director,* Australian Institute of Management, Australia

Using real-life examples and straightforward language, Guy Hale presents the success strategy of the future. Step-by-step, this book shows how effective thinking skills can translate into professional and personal triumph. Consider it required reading!

Ted Merrill, *Executive Director,* Automotive Industry Action Group

This remarkable book should have been written years ago. Thinking is not as simple as most people believe. Guy Hale pleasantly and clearly shows us how to think better to achieve a much better result. This book is a must for anybody who wishes to become a successful and better leader.

Pramukti Surjaudaja, *CEO,* Bank NISP, Jakarta

If Guy Hale's book teaches even one of my managers to think better, it will be the best investment I ever made.

Alexander Voegele, Berlin Economic Development Corporation, Berlin

A foolproof formula for success. A concise, no-nonsense, and practical step-by-step method of mentally processing information. Thanks, Guy, for taking the pain out of thinking.

Glen Tuckett, *Former Athletic Director and Baseball Coach,* Brigham Young University

The latest ideas are those that are simple and work. Guy really has some great ones here!

Les Chitester, *General Manager,* C-COR Comlux, Inc.

Thinking dominates human fate. However, few books can be found today to teach and guide people on how to think better. I personally highly recommend this book that shows you how to think in a systematic and better way.

Casper Shih, Ph.D., *President,* China Productivity Center, Taiwan

The Leader's Edge illustrates precisely why you may need to change your work habits immediately in order to protect your future.

Dave Cours, *President and CEO,* Cubic Defense Systems

This book deals with real issues that face executives quite frequently. It is easy to read with a down-to-earth basic approach to thinking clearly. It is most refreshing to see this innovative, methodical and analytical approach in print. This book is highly recommended as an investment in employees for every company and as a training method for all management levels on how to think clearly. This book will pay for itself in realized profit many times over.

Henry Mourad, *President,* CXR Telcom

It is the first book that has come across my desk with the goal of improving our thinking skills and it's about time! The book is a terrific guide to a better process for thinking that will improve our decision-making skills. We all have a continuous need to refine our ability at decision making and thus improve the efficiencies of our organization.

Southwood J. Morcott, *Chairman, President, and CEO,* Dana Corporation

The ability to manage knowledge is key to management success. Hale's book provides specific techniques discussed with real-life examples to make the processes clear.

Bob Knight, *Chairman,* Digital Sound Corporation

The innovative leader in cutting-edge training methods has done it again! Guy Hale created a fantastic blueprint on how to think effectively. A must read for everyone.

Lawrence R. Brackett, *President and CEO,* Frank Howard Allen Realtors

The Leader's Edge combines groundbreaking research with a proven blueprint for thinking better.

Lenny T. Ralphs, Ph.D., *Vice President,* Franklin Quest Co.

Guy Hale's book is a much needed contribution to the field of critical thinking. Executives who use this profound yet practical book will not only save their companies millions of dollars traditionally lost through poor thinking, but will also make their companies just as much in new opportunities.

This book is an insurance policy for those who want to maintain their competitive edge in the corporate marketplace. With these skills, you will thrive—without them you sink.

Steven A. DeVore, *President,* InteliQuest Learning Systems

I enjoyed very much this interesting and instructional reading. Fundamental for managers' information. I will buy it for all my managers and supervisors.

Antonia Carlos Queiroz, *President,* Monsanto do Brazil

I am extremely impressed with Guy's innovative approach to thinking skills that turns reactive activity into applied pro-activity.

T. Ogihara, *President,* Ogihara America Corporation

Great book! The thinking skills taught in this book are essential tools to maintain a market leadership position. One of the best books ever written on thinking.

Henry Moody, *President,* Panamax Power Protection Products

Guy's book gives new meaning to the "Paradigm Shift" concept. He presents a successful, disciplined way of thinking. He offers a new approach to assure corporate survival that transcends trendy management fads.

Dale Christensen, *President,* Pro-Log Manufacturing Service, Inc.

Sets out the kind of common sense advice that after your read it, you say, "I know that!" Question is, why don't you do it?

Hale does a great job of taking a lot of common sense skills and putting them into a practical and usable framework that can be applied both in any business as well as personal thought processes.

Mark Nielsen, *President/CEO,* Subscriber Computing, Inc.

A great book, which provides, at a time of daily information overflow, methods to focus on one's own thinking process.

Kurt F. Eise, *President,* TUV America

Solution-oriented information for today's business environment. Many good ideas to offer key managers to think more effectively.

William Versaw, *President,* Versa-Matic Pump

The Leader's Edge

Mastering the Five Skills of
Breakthrough Thinking

The Leader's Edge

Mastering
the Five
Skills of
Breakthrough
Thinking

GUY A. HALE

IRWIN
Professional Publishing

Burr Ridge, Illinois
New York, New York

Irwin Professional Book Team
Associate publisher: *Jeffery A. Krames*
Marketing managers: *Tiffany Dykes, Marissa Ramos*
Production supervisor: *Dina L Treadaway*
Project editor: *Lynne Basler*
Designer: *Michael Warrell*
Jacket designer: *Marciel Quianzon*
Compositor: *Electronic Publishing Services, Inc.*
Typeface: *11/13 Palatino*
Printer: *Quebecor Printing Book Group*

Times Mirror
Higher Education Group

Library of Congress Cataloging-in-Publication Data

Hale, Guy A.
    The leader's edge: mastering the five skills of breakthrough thinking / Guy Hale.
        p.   cm.
    Includes index.
    ISBN 0-7863-0426-X
    1. Critical thinking. 2. Problem solving. 3. Decision-making.
I. Title.
BF441.H24   1996
153.4'3—dc20   95–34290

Printed in the United States of America
1 2 3 4 5 6 7 8 9 0 Q 2 1 0 9 8 7 6 5

To the thousands of employees from all our clients who have served as the refiner's fire to develop and perfect the concepts found in *The Leader's Edge*

Preface Learning to Think in a Whole New Era

In life, as in baseball, we're constantly seeking to improve our batting average. Whatever our line of endeavor, we're all trying to raise our percentage of correct choices. I've talked to many successful CEOs about the batting average at their organization, and they usually say that 70 to 80 percent of the time their people make good judgments.

Then I ask the CEOs how often they themselves make the right calls. They say around 90 percent. So next I inquire, "What would happen if you could get your employees' percentage up to your level?" Usually, these executives roll their eyes, sigh wistfully, and say, "That would make business infinitely easier."

That's what this book is about. It will help you—and those around you—increase your batting average of correct choices. Thus, it will improve your life—and theirs.

Changing the Way We Think

Life, after all, *is* about thinking. We think about our situations or problems, at work and at home, and then we make choices. But because change is happening so much more quickly these days, how well and how fast we think has become crucial.

Doing your thinking the way you've always done it won't work as well in the future. To compete successfully, it's imperative that you learn how to think more effectively. That's because in the Information Age the traditional routes to success may no longer be effective.

Talent, for example, isn't the automatic passport to accomplishment it once was. You probably know plenty of people who are able, knowledgeable, creative, even brilliant, but are stuck in the middle of their organizations or maybe are self-employed and spinning their wheels.

Motivation, despite what the self-help gurus preach, will only get you so far. Hard work and lofty thoughts, while laudable, aren't enough unless you have the necessary skills to go with them.

Experience, long revered as a skill builder, doesn't count for as much as it used to. The work environment is changing so radically that yesterday's solutions may no longer pertain.

Even *knowledge* alone is not enough. Indeed, the knowledge available to humankind is said to be doubling every seven years. And in technical fields, half of what students learn in their freshman year of college is obsolete by the time they graduate.

So, it's not knowledge itself, but the ability to *manage* that knowledge that has become the key. And we manage knowledge by how we think.

The Hallmark of the New Leader

Recent research underscores that successful people don't just muddle along, bumping from crisis to crisis, operating from their gut instead of their head. Instead, they are clear and systemic problem solvers and decision makers. They're able to approach any situation with a proven process. They know what questions to ask, in what order, and how to act upon the answers.

In a recent CNN interview, a former U.S. Secretary of Labor was asked if he had just one shot at improving America's labor force, where he would spend federal funds. His reply was simple: "Thinking skills."

What a vast departure that is from traditional views. Only a few years ago, the answer might well have been "reading," or "computer skills," or "mathematics." But now it's "thinking."

Indeed, the hallmark of the new leader is this ability to think critically and implement proactively. Such a leader, because he or she handles information so well, can better deal with issues, not just symptoms. As organizations retrench, reorganize, and try to do more with less, such aptitude is beginning to count for more than traditional job skills.

Even Nations

It's almost impossible to exaggerate the importance of our way of thinking. How we think influences people, organizations, even nations. Japan's economic ascendancy in the last few decades, for example, was a direct result of how its people think. The Japanese invest heavily in doing things right the first time and in dissecting the best of what already exists to devise an even better product.

The American mind, on the other hand, is more inclined to get something produced quickly and then improve it on the fly. Americans at their core believe there will always be time to fix things, make improvements, and do whatever is needed to win in the end. This is an increasingly outmoded view.

Not only logic and efficiency but, increasingly, economic survival is dictating the need for better thinking skills. The task of rationalizing American business is becoming urgent. For example, ISO 9000, an international standard of quality management, is rapidly taking hold in the United States. It requires organizations to address basic quality issues in order to develop consistency in their business processes while meeting customers' needs. The idea is that you must have a rational basis to run your business on, or quality will ultimately suffer.

So thinking is quickly becoming a matter of dollars and sense. I've had business executives tell me how a single instance of using one of the skills explained in this book has saved them $15 million or more by forcing them to organize an orderly attack on issues rather than going off half-cocked.

The Only Lasting Advantage

There's only one lasting competitive advantage available to a person or an organization. That's the ability to think more clearly and implement more quickly. Just *how* powerful is the lure of such skills? A few years ago, I was teaching 25 executives from Fortune 500 firms, and the session was going, I thought, particularly well. The energy of the group was high, and I seemed to be reaching everyone.

Much to my surprise, though, a successful, young vice president from one of the nation's leading investment-banking firms came up to me and said, "Guy, I've decided not to recommend this training to my company."

I was stunned. "Why not?" I asked.

He smiled. "I've learned so much in this seminar that I'll be able to dominate my peers when it comes to making the best recommendations, implementing them, and selling my way of thinking. Why would I want my colleagues to know these skills? I'll advance much faster if I'm the only one in my company who knows how to use them."

Enough said! We both laughed, and he went back to his firm, which has since sent many others to my thinking-skills seminars.

The Crucible of Experience

I've spent more than 20 years teaching the principles of thinking to business and government leaders from General Motors to Hewlett-Packard and from Australia to Germany. And I've distilled these skills down to five uncomplicated processes.

These skills have been fire tested in the crucible of practical experience. CEOs use them to solve billion-dollar problems involving thousands of people, while scientists apply them when working alone in the lab. Merger-and-acquisition specialists employ these skills to make the best deals, and companies use them to choose key personnel. Thousands of individuals rely on the five thinking skills for personal concerns like deciding where to go for a summer vacation or how to help select a college for their kids.

Regardless of the situation, the skills themselves remain constant. Only the information changes. So you can count on the thinking skills to bring clarity and order during stressful times. Properly used, they will not fail you. Master them, and you're likely to have a more successful career, make better business decisions, and be happier in your personal life.

Steering through Troubled Waters

There are five skills, the first of which (Situation Review) unites all the others.

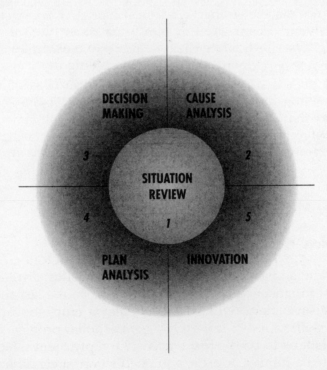

When conditions are murky and confusing, you use Situation Review (Skill No. 1) to help you separate and prioritize the concerns. Then you decide, one by one, which of the other four thinking skills to use with each of those concerns.

Cause Analysis (Skill No. 2) comes into play when the task is to find out what went wrong while Decision Making (Skill No. 3) helps you choose among alternatives. Put Plan Analysis (Skill No. 4) into action when the situation requires coming up with a way to implement a decision. Or if what's involved is conceiving a whole new approach to an issue, that's the time to use Innovation (Skill No. 5).

These skills may be familiar to you. That's because everyone already uses some of these skills to some degree. But rarely do I find anyone who uses them as well as they could. So I'll try to systemize them in such a way that you will be more able to apply them fully and consistently, making the right decisions more of the time and thus improving your batting average.

Do you believe, as most do, that you're already an expert thinker? You may be wrong. As a test, you might have yourself and others in your organization or family sit down with a pen and paper and describe how they solve problems, make decisions, and plan. The response can be telling.

Most people use the same approach regardless of whether they're solving problems, making decisions, or planning. If your people say that's how they address a concern, you'll know you will all benefit greatly from this book. And if they can't describe how they make a decision—if they say they "just do it"—then thank your lucky stars you're still around! A lack of thinking skills has killed more than a few organizations.

A Practical Guide

This book will give you a good understanding of the five thinking skills. But to make it as practical as possible, in the last two chapters I'll also explain two other concepts to help you apply the thinking skills.

One is how to be the best advocate for your ideas. No matter how skilled a thinker you are, you need to persuade others before you can put your thoughts and ideas into effect (Chapter 6).

The other is how to teach the thinking skills to others. Helping others along that path will pay off for years to come for you, your family, or your organization (Chapter 7). In Chapter 8, you will learn how to master one of life's greatest challenges—people problems.

This book aims to be a hands-on guide, written in reader-friendly language, and filled with frequent anecdotes and hypotheticals having the ring of reality. In fact, all the anecdotes are based on *actual situations* I've encountered while working with organizations. Thus, I'll place you in complex situations where costs, people issues, internal political problems, and personal concerns are no strangers. Then I'll show you how you can bring order to chaos. Decades of on-the-job experience may teach you exactly these same skills, but you don't have to wait that long. And you can avoid some of the bruises you're sure to encounter along the way.

I want to help you improve the way you process information by the way you think. By perfecting the uses of the five skills described in this book you'll have a leg up. You'll improve your personal power, be less stressed, and naturally become a leader of others. Not necessarily a leader in the traditional sense, but a new leader by today's standard—leading yourself and others toward better handling of knowledge in the Information Age.

Acknowledgments

I would like to thank the following people for their support in writing this book:

Margret McBride, my agent, for helping me through the business side.

Dale Fetherling for his valuable assistance in putting my thoughts and ideas into the format for this book.

Mark Morton, the "genius in charge of Product Development at Alamo Learning Systems; his contributions have transformed the technology of the thinking skills into an artistic format.

Lanette Miller, who fought the fires and helped manage me so that I had the time to write.

Lance Hale for taking over many of my responsibilities and showing me that others can do what I do—even better.

And to all who wish to maximize their success in the Information Age.

Contents

Mastering the 5 Skills

DECISION MAKING

CAUSE ANALYSIS

3

2

SITUATION REVIEW

4

1

5

PLAN ANALYSIS

INNOVATION

Each of the next five chapters will put you at the center of a realistic situation—and then help you navigate through it using one of the five thinking skills. You'll learn what questions to ask, in what order, and then how to act upon those answers.

Master these skills, and you'll be able to approach any situation or problem with a proven skill and process. As a result, your response time will improve, you'll be more effective, and you will have a greater confidence in everything you do.

Chapter **One**

Skill 1 Situation Review
Clearing the Fog

Given the rigors of the recent bank reorganization, Mark's two-week vacation in Jamaica with his fiancée was wonderful and long overdue. But now it's his first day back as the newly appointed Executive Vice President of Operations, and his sense of relaxation is disappearing faster than his tan.

Mark has hardly settled behind his desk when he learns that:

- Human Resources is behind schedule in reducing head-count in targeted departments. Another 5 percent has to be cut in the next six months beyond the 5 percent already pared. "We haven't been able to figure out how we're going to do this," the manager tells Mark.

- Sales and Marketing says the reorganization upheaval is affecting morale. "It seems as if some people don't really care about the quality of the work they do," Mark is told. "In fact, they don't seem to care about *anything*. I'm afraid this attitude may filter out to our customers. We have to do something about this—*now!*"

- Customer Service is complaining about a chronic computer problem that increasingly makes check retrieval impossible, irritating customers and employees alike.

- A companywide task force has put a report on Mark's desk about a proposed new, $10-million information system. But the sharply divided task force bumped an actual decision up to him because it could not agree on department issues and who gets served first.

- The bank president has sent a memo to top-level staff members informing them of a change in a neighboring state's banking laws that could open opportunities there. He then specifically tells Mark he expects him to lead the effort to come up with new tactics that would allow the bank to siphon lucrative business from the established banks there.

As if that weren't enough, Madeline, Mark's executive assistant, a very able employee who is pregnant with her first child, isn't feeling well and wants to leave early. But she says that before she leaves, she urgently needs to talk to him about her "personal situation."

Mark nods, forces a pleasant smile. "Give me a chance to dig out from under some of this," he says to Madeline, pointing to his cluttered desk, "and then we'll try to find a moment to talk."

Inwardly, though, Mark groans. He is sure Madeline wants to ask about starting her maternity leave early, meaning he'll have to tackle all these projects without her help. Further, Mark has heard that Charley, an assistant to the bank president as well as Mark's rival and nemesis, played tennis with the bank president several times while Mark was in Jamaica. What could he be up to?

For just a moment, it all seems too much. Mark wishes he were back on the beach at Ocho Rios with his toughest decision being whether to apply sunblock before or after snorkeling.

But then he takes a deep breath and regains his confidence. After all, he's learned how to think perfectly. He knows he has the leader's edge. So if he attacks these issues with proven skills, if he is calm and analytical, if he's proactive, he *can* do this. I've done it before, he says to himself, and I can do it again.

Then the phone rings. It's Mark's fiancée, Suzanne, who's also a vice president, but at another bank. She asks how his day's going. After he ticks off his business crises for her one by one, Suzanne says, "I'm not sure how you can remember all those problems, let alone solve them. But guess what? You've got *another* one."

She pauses, then continues, "Today I was told I'm being considered for a promotion. It's a great job and one I really want, but, unfortunately, it would involve a transfer to another state. Already, the prospect of leaving is tearing me up. This one is going to be a tough call for me. Really, for *us*. But let's not discus it right now. Let's set aside some time tonight to talk, okay?"

"I'll try," Mark said. "I'm not sure when yet, but I'll try to make time tonight."

A Bedrock Principle

Even without his concerns about Madeline, Charley, and Suzanne, Mark's bundle of banking issues would be intimidating for any executive. But such business concerns—intertwined, interdepartmental, and often of indeterminate origin—are increasingly common today as firms cut back, reengineer, and try to do more with less.

So, why does Mark feel so sure of himself? Why, after just a bit of initial anxiety, does he feel the pressure lifting?

For one thing, it sure was nice to take a moment's break and talk to Suzanne about the concerns. That lifted his spirits. More important, Mark remembered a bedrock principle from his training in the thinking skills: *There is no concern that can't be resolved by one of the thinking skills.* Armed with those skills, Mark is less likely to become rattled and much more likely to get the projects moving, provide value to his organization, be a leader to his subordinates, and be a rising star in the eyes of his superiors.

Before plunging into the morass, Mark takes another deep breath and reviews the issues. What we have here, he says to himself, is a tangled mass of issues. But where do I start? What can be done now? How can I get control over all these moving parts?

This is a case, he decides, for Situation Review, Skill No. 1.

Mark's problem is not uncommon. Issues in any organization are often ponderous, and at first glance, unmanageable. And, for that matter, issues in any family can be just as knotty. Anyone who's raised children can attest that business doesn't have a monopoly on difficult, multiple concerns. The deadlines, cost, internal politics, and, of course, personal factors can be equally common and burdensome as those Mark faces.

But whether such concerns occur at work or at home, Situation Review comes into play first. Situation Review, you might say, is the Rosetta Stone of thinking skills: It unlocks the secret of how to deal with cases that seem overwhelmingly complex in the new information age where accuracy and speed are absolutely critical for survival. Situation Review involves sorting out the concerns, setting priorities, and getting started on solutions.

It's the linchpin of clear thinking because it's not only a valuable skill in itself, it also shows you how to employ the other four thinking skills. If you master Situation Review, the other principles of the thinking skills will be more obvious and easier to apply, and unwieldy situations will become eminently workable.

Taking One Step at a Time

Most crises, as our friend Mark discerned, aren't monolithic. They're mosaics, with each situation really consisting of a number of smaller issues. *The only way anyone manages his or her way out of what looks like a grand mess is by taking one step at a time—or, as they say, the only way to eat an elephant is one bite at a time.*

So it's imperative to learn what those individual issues are. That takes some discipline, some analytical skill, some innovation, and some time. There's a tendency, especially among aggressive leaders, to want to blast through tough situations, issue orders right and left, and show that they're fighting the foe. American organizations have traditionally rewarded this style of leadership.

However, unless you've figured out what the foe is and how best to dispatch it, this frenetic effort is likely to be more sizzle than steak. Further, it might worsen the situation. The leader that leads calmly, not chaotically, eventually becomes the natural leader in the new information age.

Our friend Mark, for instance, might be tempted to get started on his series of concerns by immediately selecting the criteria for choosing the new information system. That appears more clear-cut than some of the other concerns. So at least he could reduce his headaches by one. But, as we'll see, that wouldn't be wise.

Instead, what Mark does (and what you should do when facing a similar host of concerns) is first show the resolve to slow down for as long as it takes, be that an hour or so, and assess the situation. Here's what you'll find:

- Not all concerns are critical.
- Not everything needs to be addressed at once.
- There is a preferred first action.

Sounds reasonable, you say. But how do you begin?
Well, there are four steps. They're logical and easy to remember.

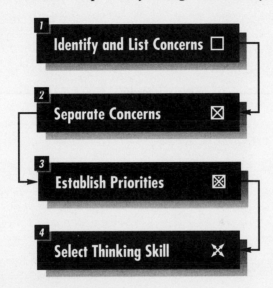

STEP ONE

The first step is to itemize all concerns. What's a "concern"? Let's look at a couple of simple definitions.

Situation

A situation is an event, a happening, or a description of same. An example would be that memo from the bank president saying that he wants to invade competing turf in a neighboring state.

Concern

A concern is a description of a person's *need* to take action on or pay attention to a particular situation. People convert a situation to a concern by identifying their own need to act. In Mark's case, the boss's memo might have been a situation earlier today. But once Mark was picked to head the effort, suddenly this issue became a *major* concern.

As you can see, a leader must constantly review *situations* to see if they affect him or her, to see if they are really *concerns*. A leader who doesn't know what's happening won't be able to anticipate the need for action. He or she will lose the chance to be proactive and will just have to respond to events.

Good leaders have well-honed sensing systems that help them detect concerns long before they become crises. The first step in Situation Review, then, is to list those concerns.

A cautionary note: When making your list, avoid verbs like *review, discuss,* and *investigate.* Those describe the activity, not the result. Instead, to be proactive, state the concern in terms of what you want the end result to be. That's really your goal. You don't wish to "review progress on your new product launch." You want to "find out what's needed to keep the new product launch on schedule."

Getting a Handle on the Situation

Back to our friend Mark and his megaconcerns.

Using Situation Review, he first needs to list his concerns so he can get a handle on all of them. He sits down with pen and paper and makes a list.

	Concerns
●	✓ Reduce headcounts in all targeted departments
	✓ Morale is poor in Sales and Marketing
	✓ Find the source of Customer Service's computer problems
	✓ Decide on criteria for new information system
	✓ Figure out how to develop business in adjacent state

Mark is pleased with the list. He doesn't know how he is going to accomplish all of this. He doesn't yet know which of the five concerns he should tackle first or how to approach any of them. But at least he *does* know what he's dealing with, what his concerns are.

Not yet on the list, but simmering in the back of Mark's mind, are these questions: Can he get away early enough to have the career talk with Suzanne? Where will he find time to discuss Madeline's "personal situation"? If Madeline wants to start her maternity leave immediately, can he afford to let her go?

On top of that, Mark wonders what, if anything, he should do to counter Charley's apparent politicking with the bank president. (Charley wanted the vice president's job that Mark got, and he's reportedly been telling the president that the bank's problems may career out of control if Mark remains in charge of all operations.)

Mark decides those are *real* concerns, too, affecting his ability to do his job today. So he decides to treat them that way by adding them to his list of concerns. He expands his list.

Concerns

- ✓ Reduce headcounts in all targeted departments
- ✓ Morale is poor in Sales and Marketing
- ✓ Find the source of Customer Service's computer problems
- ✓ Decide on criteria for new information system
- ✓ Figure out how to develop business in adjacent state
- ✓ Decide if I can get away early enough tonight to meet Suzanne
- ✓ Decide if I can find time today to talk to Madeline
- ✓ Decide if Madeline can start pregnancy leave early, if requested
- ✓ Determine what to do, if anything, about Charley

STEP TWO

Separate Concerns   ☒

Often a concern is quite clear, for instance, the third item on Mark's list: "Find source of Customer Service's computer problems." If all the concerns can be as simply stated, the leader can skip this step and go on to Step Three: Establish Priorities.

But many times a concern is vaguely stated or is stated in such a way that several issues are entwined. If so, Step Two is needed to break a concern into manageable pieces. Otherwise, you might waste time trying for that impossibly magic solution that solves all concerns at once.

Separate Concerns

For example, one large company was worried about the high turnover of its professional employees. Upon further study, however, it found that there were really two concerns: the turnover of new employees and the departure of older professionals. Many members of both groups were leaving, and all the departures were costly. But the younger employees and the older employees each had different needs, and there were different reasons for their lack of loyalty. Each part of the turnover concern required a different solution.

At other times, the exact nature of the concern is vague. For example, "We have a communication problem." That's a common kind of generalized statement, one that can't be managed in that form. It has to be separated into manageable pieces: Executives never have time to attend meetings, and the internal e-mail system never has worked right.

Or there might be confusion because several concerns are combined in one statement, such as, "We need to decide on the marketing, pricing, and packaging for our new product." These can't be treated as single, manageable concerns. They must be broken down so they can be analyzed individually.

A Key Question

A key question in all these cases—and the way to determine if Step Two of Situation Review is really needed—is will *one* action, *one* cause, or *one* decision be sufficient to explain or resolve this concern? If the answer is no, separation is required.

In the case of beleaguered Mark at the bank, he looks again at his list of nine concerns: headcount reduction, bad morale, computer problem, information-systems criteria, concepts for new territory, meeting with Suzanne, meeting with Madeline, Madeline's pregnancy leave, and Charley's politicking.

"*Whew*! That's a lot of concerns," Mark says to himself. But he calmly studies them and concludes that eight of the nine appear to stand alone. Each of those eight concerns requires only one decision or one effort at fact-finding, analysis, or imagination.

Which concern requires more than that? The "morale" concern. It's too vaguely stated. It's a generalized description, not a statement of a concern on which action can be taken.

So it's appropriate to ask further questions about it:

- What do we mean by "morale" concern?
- In what ways is poor morale manifesting itself?
- What else is wrong that could cause poor morale?

These questions help reduce a complex, murky concern to its essence. Until that's done, it really can't be dealt with logically.

That's why we can say unequivocally: *No leader in history has ever solved a "morale problem" per se!* If it was solved, it was because the leader reduced the "morale" concern to its components and then fixed those.

So Mark sees that more investigation is going to be needed before he can tackle the Sales and Marketing morale question. Meanwhile, by asking questions, he finds that many Sales and Marketing employees fear for their jobs because of a false belief that their department is going to suffer exceptionally heavy losses under the headcount-reduction program. In fact, the rumor has so dispirited the department that sales production has fallen and because of that bank revenues may be down for the quarter.

In addition to fears about the headcount reduction, someone in Sales and Marketing got access to purported salary figures at the bank's corporate office and passed them around. Thus, many Sales and Marketing people are further upset because they believe they are underpaid relative to their workload and that of their counterparts on the corporate staff.

Mark mulls this over and restates the morale concern as follows:

- Explain to Sales and Marketing that it's not targeted for disproportionate losses under the headcount-reduction program.
- Decide if Sales and Marketing's compensation needs adjustment.

Mark revises his list of concerns. Each now seems to stand alone. Each requires one decision or one effort at fact-finding, analysis, or imagination. The new list looks like this:

Concerns

●	✓ Reduce headcounts in all targeted departments
	✓ Communicate to Sales and Marketing that they are not targeted for disproportionate reductions in force
	✓ Decide if Sales and Marketing's compensation needs adjustment
	✓ Find the source of Customer Service's computer problems
	✓ Decide on criteria for new information system
	✓ Figure out how to develop business in adjacent state
●	✓ Decide if I can get away early enough tonight to meet Suzanne
	✓ Decide if I can find time today to talk to Madeline
	✓ Decide if Madeline can start pregnancy leave early, if requested
	✓ Determine what to do, if anything, about Charley

Mark is pleased with his list. It has grown in length—but also in clarity. He now has 10 clear concerns to attack. But he still doesn't know which of them to attack first. So he very much needs the next step.

STEP THREE

Establish Priorities

Having listed our concerns and, if necessary, broken them into manageable pieces, we are now ready to take some action.

But *what* action? And which do we attack *first*?

Reasonable people can disagree on such questions. What's most important to one person may be less so to another. There are many ways to set priorities, and nothing can replace the individual leader's judgment.

However, there are some obvious criteria that can be used to help arrange the facts in a rational way. A typical list of factors for defining importance would include the following:

- Impact/seriousness.
- Urgency/timing.
- Potential payoff.
- Resources required.
- Time estimate for resolution.

Successful people would consider all of these in setting priorities. For simplicity's sake, I suggest you take the criteria you feel are most important and use them as a basic standard. Usually a minimal list of criteria would include the following questions:

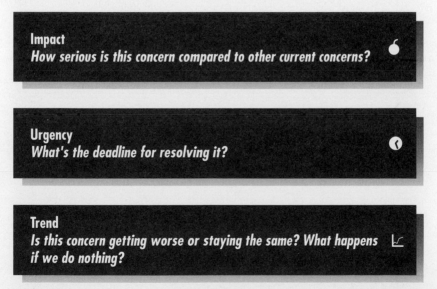

Impact
How serious is this concern compared to other current concerns?

Urgency
What's the deadline for resolving it?

Trend
Is this concern getting worse or staying the same? What happens if we do nothing?

By considering at least those three factors, you should be able to get a sense of what requires immediate attention and what can be deferred.

Here are some important guidelines to use when setting such priorities:

- All rankings are based on *relative* impact, *relative* urgency, *relative* trend. These concerns must be compared to one another, not to some optimal environment and not to last year's or last month's concern.

- In the real world, many concerns may seem equally serious. But it's important here to rank them in descending order of priority so that your plan of attack is absolutely clear.

- Some concerns, while not as weighty as others, must be handled *sooner*. That increases their relative priority. In fact, you should attach deadlines to all concerns so that you'll be sure to monitor progress.

- All rankings must be based on information, not opinion. There should be discussion, not just conjecture, about why, for example, turnover among older professionals has more, or less, impact than does turnover among newer employees.

Getting back to banker Mark and his concerns, he earlier listed his 10 concerns. Now he needs to prioritize them.

Rather than just guessing or stating his own opinion, he talks to the people involved. He finds out some interesting information. For one thing, the law changing banking regulations in the neighboring state—the concern that has the boss so excited—has passed, but it actually won't take effect for another 18 months. So, although meeting that challenge is probably as important for Mark's career as it is for the bank, he thinks he can defer action.

The question of the criteria for the new information systems may be connected to that as well. If the bank is going to expand into the neighboring state in a big way, that could change its whole operation and might make new, costly information systems almost immediately obsolete. Though making a choice among the criteria shouldn't be all that difficult for Mark, he again decides there is an advantage to waiting awhile.

The "morale" question in Sales and Marketing—now broken down into information and money issues—looms more immediate. Already revenues may be at risk which is sure to get the attention of corporate staff and the Board of Directors. Besides, it's believed that customers are beginning to detect the department's malaise. Anything that can affect the bank's image and its customer service gets a top priority from Mark.

The overall headcount-reduction question obviously is important, especially if unfounded fears and rumors abound elsewhere as they do among the Sales and Marketing staff. So there's logic in trying to get this program nailed down and then announced.

The computer problem in Customer Service is another issue with repercussions for the customers. If they need to see back checks and can't get them, they're going to be upset. So that one, too, rates high on Mark's list.

The question of whether he can meet with Suzanne at an appointed time obviously isn't of the same business magnitude as the other concerns, but it must be decided within a few hours. Similarly, the two Madeline questions will have relatively little impact on the bank but must be addressed soon. On the other hand, the concerns of Charley's politicking could be very important for Mark's future, but probably isn't something that has to be handled immediately.

Once again, Mark sits down, lists his concerns and using this new knowledge, maps out the impact/urgency/trend of the 10 issues, with "1" indicating highest, "3" lowest. Then in the last column, he factors in the need to act quickly on some of the lesser concerns. He assigns a final, or overall, priority and his list now looks like this:

Concerns

	Impact	Urgency	Trend	Final Priority
✓ Reduce headcounts	2	2	1	7
✓ Communicate facts about Sales & Mktng attrition	1	2	1	4
✓ Decide about Sales and Marketing's compensation	1	3	1	5
✓ Find computer glitch	1	2	1	6
✓ Decide criteria	2	3	3	8
✓ Develop out-of-state concepts	1	3	3	9
✓ Decide Suzanne meeting	1	2	3	3
✓ Decide Madeline meeting	2	1	1	1
✓ Decide Madeline leave	2	1	2	2
✓ Determine response to Charley	1	3	3	10

Mark feels good about his list. The order in which the concerns need to be attacked is now clear. In fact, some of the most imminent concerns, such as the Suzanne and Madeline meetings, will be resolved within a few hours.

Among the weightier concerns, the two-part Sales and Marketing "morale" problem and the Customer Service computer issue have a high priority because they can affect customers as well as employees and, left unchecked, could hurt the bank's financial future.

The out-of-state banking concern looms large for the future. But resolving that will take some study and fortunately there is some flexibility on time. Both the headcount reduction and the information-systems criteria may be affected by what is decided about the out-of-state banking question. So those three concerns can be grouped together on the middle burner.

Mark can't rest easy by any means. He's got a lot of work to do—and everybody's watching! But he knows now that it's all doable. He won't be running around helter-skelter trying to put out fires. He has figured out how the various issues are entwined and in what order they need to be attacked.

In fact, just listing the concerns and their priority has been a catharsis. Several issues already are more clear because of his understanding of their relationship to each other. For instance, if the bank president knew Mark has a logical plan for how to proceed, that could be a plus in dealing with Charley's maneuvering.

So Mark decides he will be proactive. He'll make an appointment with the president for tomorrow morning to give him a progress report and, not so coincidentally, counter Charley in a positive way. That's not the total solution to the Charley issue, but it's a step in the right direction.

Getting his concerns on track also produces another breakthrough for Mark. He sees that he should be able to get away tonight for the talk with Suzanne. He calls her and brings her up to date. "Yes, let's definitely plan to have that talk tonight, Suzanne. That's going to be a big decision. We're going to need to spend some time and think through this clearly."

Mark is making such progress that he also decides he *does* have time right now to talk to Madeline. He calls her in. He was right! She wants to take her maternity leave early, starting next week. "Can I *do* that," she asks with a worried look, "given all the work we've got ahead of us?"

Mark nods and smiles again. Another issue falls to the wayside because he's feeling confident of his thinking and his planning. "Don't worry, Madeline. We'll shortly have everything under control. Take all the time you need. You *deserve* it—and so does that baby!"

Madeline, beaming, thanks Mark profusely. "What a great boss!" she says to herself. Mark, then, goes to Step Four.

STEP FOUR

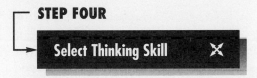

Like most leaders, Mark began with uncertainty about the concerns. But he wisely avoided the temptation to charge headlong into the fray and make decisions that he might later regret. Instead, armed with a proven system of thinking skills, Mark took the time to assess the situation.

Deciding that the problem called for Situation Review, he first identified, clarified, and separated the concerns. Then he established priorities for each. Now he must decide how best to resolve them.

To accomplish this, the leader needs to ask himself or herself, What do I *want* when I'm through analyzing?

- To find a cause?
- To make a choice?
- To develop or improve on a plan?
- To come up with a whole new concept?

We will delve into each of these four thinking skills in the next four chapters. But, for now, understand these basics:

- If your aim is to find what's causing a problem, you will want to use *Cause Analysis*.

- If you are looking to choose among alternatives, your next step is *Decision Making*.

- If what's involved is ensuring the success of a decision already made, you will want to employ *Plan Analysis*.

- If what you've got is a concern that requires a totally new creative concept, the skill is called *Innovation*.

Choosing among the Thinking Skills

Mark looks over his newly prioritized list of remaining concerns and considers which thinking skill to use with each and what the timetable should be.

His list looks like this, in descending order of urgency:

Concerns

	Purpose	Deadline
• ~~1. Decide Madeline meeting~~	~~Make a choice~~	~~Today~~
~~2. Decide Madeline leave~~	~~Make a Choice~~	~~Today~~
~~3. Decide Suzanne meeting~~	~~Make a Choice~~	~~Today~~
4. Communicate facts about Sales & Mktng. attrition	Develop Plan	Tomorrow
• 5. Decide about Sales & Marketing's compensation	Make a Choice	48 hours
6. Find computer glitch	Find a Cause	7 days
7. Reduce headcounts	Develop Plan	10 days
8. Decide criteria	Make a Choice	1 month
9. Develop out-of-state concepts	Conceive New Ideas	3 months
10. Determine response to Charley	Make a Choice	6 months

There! Mark has already resolved three of his concerns and stated clear objectives and deadlines for the others. Those objectives, in turn, will tell him which of the thinking skills to employ.

Mark needs to put out accurate information to Sales and Marketing about staff cuts. If he does it with say a memo, he must then plan what he's going to say, and how he's going to say it. So that's a case for Plan Analysis.

Whether compensation schedules should be changed for Sales and Marketing requires a choice: Recommendation A, B, or C. Thus, it calls for Decision Making.

Mark sees that the computer glitch that's troubling Customer Service is a case for Cause Analysis because the need is to find out what keeps going wrong and why. Getting the companywide head-count reduction back on track means Plan Analysis because what's needed is a way to implement the targeted reduction in force.

The concern of the criteria for a new information system is ready-made for Decision Making because it involves making choices. The president's desire for some new ideas from Mark about how to invade banking turf in another state calls for coming up with a whole new approach. So that calls for Innovation.

And, while Mark has taken a first step toward resolving the Charley question, clearly that's going to take a sustained effort. So he needs to develop a plan by using Plan Analysis.

Mark completes his list of remaining issues like this:

Concerns

	Priority	Thinking Skill
1. Communicate facts about Sales & Mktng. attrition	1 (Tomorrow)	Plan Analysis
2. Decide about Sales & Marketing's compensation	2 (48 hours)	Decision Making
3. Find computer glitch	3 (7 days)	Cause Analysis
4. Reduce headcounts	4 (10 days)	Plan Analysis
5. Decide criteria	5 (1 month)	Decision Making
6. Develop out-of-state concepts	6 (3 months)	Innovation
7. Determine response to Charley	7 (6 months)	Decision Making

Mark emits a huge sigh of relief as he puts his feet up on the desk and ponders how much he has accomplished in just one day back on the job. Using Situation Review, he was able to quickly get a handle on problems that just a few hours earlier seemed about to veer out of control.

Mark at this point also can consider which of the concerns can best be delegated. For example, the question of the compensation for the Sales and Marketing staff is one that Mark may want to hand off to the human resource manager. The headcount-reduction concern might benefit by having an outside consultant take a look at the current plan and make suggestions. The interstate banking concern is another one on which an outside viewpoint might be useful.

Mark takes another deep, satisfied breath. Now, far from running scared, he's in firm command. Mark now knows what the concerns are, what the urgency of each is, how he is going to attack them and by when, and which ones he may wish to delegate. He still must follow through, of course. But now that he's comfortable with the nature of the challenges, he's *ready* for them.

He's made an appointment to see the bank president tomorrow to fill him in on the progress. Mark feels sure that the quick way he grasped the concerns and plotted his attack is the kind of accomplishment the bank president will admire, the kind that will put Charley's self-serving posturing into perspective.

A Lot Like Playing Golf

Situation Review doesn't itself solve problems. But it will help you sort them out, rank their importance and urgency, and label them according to the desired result.

When faced with a particularly complex or murky situation or, as was true in Mark's case, when there are so many things happening that it's difficult to know where to start, that's the time to back off, catch your breath, and do a Situation Review.

In fact, you might think of Situation Review as being a lot like playing golf. Getting around the golf course, naturally, involves a series of hurdles, or challenges.

What makes the game intriguing is that those challenges vary from course to course and from hole to hole on any given course. The best golfer is often the one who is the most versatile and who makes the best decisions, as well as the best execution, at each juncture.

At one point, your challenge as a golfer is the need for a long, high drive over a lake. Then, it's a chip shot up the hill, out of the rough, and onto the green. A moment later, it's a tricky putt that's got your attention. You use a different club and different skills for each of these shots.

The analogy applies to life as well: You don't use the same thinking skill to resolve every issue you face. Or if you do, you're going to be as effective as the duffer who uses a three iron off the tee while his competitors have high-tech drivers with graphite shafts.

Situation Review allows you to match the right "club" with the right challenge. Again, the way to do that is to go through these four steps:

- **Step 1**: List the concerns.
- **Step 2**: Separate concerns into smaller parts (if needed).
- **Step 3**: Set priorities and timetables.
- **Step 4**: Decide which skills you'll use to resolve each.

The goal of Situation Review is to think through what needs to be done in a way that allows you to tackle the *right* concerns, in the *right* order, with the *right* skill, and for the *right* reasons.

Mark, confident he's on the right track, calls Suzanne again. Yes, he confirms, he'll be there, not only on time but in good spirits and ready to help her come to grips with her job situation and how it may affect them.

"You seem awfully upbeat," she says.

"I *am*. I've moved mountains today."

"You got all those work problems solved?"

"Well, if not solved, at least sorted out and on the path to being solved."

"How in the world did you do that so quickly?"

"You'll see," Mark says. "You'll see tonight."

"*What?* What will I see?"

"You'll see me. Then you'll see how much I care for you."

"How will I know how much?"

Mark chuckles. "Because I'll bring flowers and, as an added bonus, the secrets of the Thinking Skills. With them, we can sort out *our* situation."

Chapter **Two**

Skill 2 Cause Analysis
Getting to the Root Cause

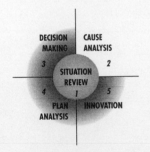

Your sales manager, Loren, did so well in nailing down that big contract that you decide to treat him to a Mexican lunch at a popular local restaurant. You both have a grand time. Except that Loren later gets sick and has to leave work early.

Meanwhile, you're fine. You wonder why he became ill, and you try to remember who ordered what. Let's see...you shared chips and guacamole. You both had ice water. You each had lemonade. You and Loren split a side order of rice and beans, and you both ate corn, not flour, tortillas.

But Loren had a beef burrito, while you had the chicken enchilada. Aha! The entree was the only different item on Loren's menu. So a bad burrito *could* have been the cause of his sudden illness. Congratulations! You've just used deductive logic, comparative problem solving.

You started with a *problem.* A problem is a deviation from a standard (in this case, feeling ill) with an unknown cause (probably something eaten). Then you identified the *facts* (what you each ate). Then you did a *comparison* (pinpointing the difference in menus) and arrived at a likely cause. Voila! Or, in this case, *bien hecho!*

23

It's just that easy and natural when the facts are simple. But while the process is easy to understand, the facts can be very complex in modern life, so complex that it takes knowledge and discipline to thoroughly review them all and make accurate comparisons.

The Role of Change

Most, if not all, problems result from change. If nothing changes, a situation remains status quo.

Isaac Newton postulated something to the effect that a body in motion tends to continue moving in the same direction unless acted upon by an outside force. That's a critical principle in Cause Analysis and is shown graphically in the following diagram.

Negative Deviation

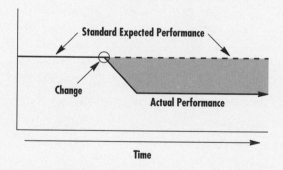

Common sense tells us that somehow, somewhere, something changed in or around the point at which the divergence becomes visible. The puzzled leader often guesses at the cause, then acts on that hunch. Trial and error substitutes for genuine analysis.

But in this chapter, we'll see how a top-flight manager, like a top-flight detective, can strip away a mystery and get to the bottom of things. I'll show you how to identify key changes, verify which one is causing the problem, then set about correcting it.

You'll learn to differentiate among symptoms and effects and to ask the right questions to find out the root cause of problems.

An Enormous Payoff

The payoff for knowing and using this process can be enormous. A very successful manufacturer of electronic test equipment, for example, was stunned when suddenly 60 percent of its products were breaking down once they were installed by customers.

The firm's reputation and profits, perhaps even its survival, were seriously threatened. Its leaders were stymied because no single part was failing consistently. The company eventually did a Cause Analysis, which ruled out operator error and poor materials. Instead, it was discovered that a few bottles of cleaning solution in which the parts were bathed had been mislabeled, and that the solution in those bottles was corrosive. As a result of this successful Cause Analysis, the firm began chemical control on its assembly line and was able to practically eliminate product failures in the field.

Cause Analysis can be used in many kinds of situations, not just technical or manufacturing puzzles. Problems can include such nontechnical problems as these:

- A department that's running overbudget.
- Health care applications that are being processed too slowly.
- Someone's behavior becoming erratic.
- An employee-assistance program that's mistrusted.
- A retail chain that's not achieving its growth goals.
- A career that has not turned out as expected.

And, in fact, Cause Analysis can even be used when there's a *positive* deviation, that is, when there's a good kind of "problem." For example, if one assembly line begins producing 500 units per hour instead of the usual 400, you'd want to know why so you could sustain that pace and maybe export it to other areas of the organization.

In all cases, just as you did with the simple scenario of the Mexican lunch, you will want to (1) define the problem, (2) study the differences and changes, and (3) compare and contrast the facts to get at the most likely cause.

In this chapter, then, we'll look at how to reconstruct the past, dispel the mystery, and find out the cause of the problem using the following process:

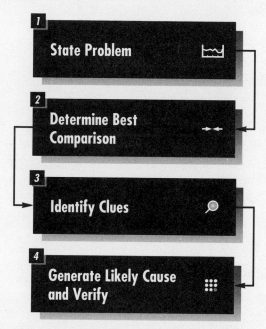

Among the key questions a leader needs to ask are these:

- What has gone wrong?
- What sets this problem apart from others?
- What, if anything, has changed?
- What are the likely causes?
- How will you verify the cause?

Again, it sounds simple. And it *is*. Or at least, the process is. But, as you're about to see, the issues in a real-life case can pose an immense challenge.

The Case of the Troublesome Pager

You're the president of Beker Communication, and you're upset. Customer complaints about your new Beker-9 Mini-Pager began coming in only a few weeks after the introduction some nine months ago of the ultra-lightweight, versatile pager.

You had such high hopes for the Beker-9. You were proud of its advanced, easy-to-use switch and the built-in calculator that's proven popular with engineers, managers, scientists, construction supervisors, and others who must work with figures while in the field.

Now, as you wait for your top staff to arrive for an emergency meeting on the Beker-9 problem, you leaf through the preliminary reports. You don't like what you see:

- Complaints have risen steadily, now representing almost 20 percent of the pagers shipped.

- To make things worse, the pagers don't just stop working. They fail intermittently—sometimes receiving, sometimes not—before halting completely. This frustrates users even more than a totally dead pager would.

- A large construction outfit has just returned more than half its 300 units, and now a big grain elevator company, whose president is a personal friend of yours, is canceling future orders. That hurts! But, on the other hand, a cola manufacturer has had great success with its Beker-9s and wants more of them. This inconsistency doesn't make any sense.

- Not only is Beker being hurt in the pager marketplace, your people are spending more time handling disgruntled customers and tracking down problems than they are selling. So sales of other Beker products are being affected, as is overall morale and efficiency.

- Your quality-control people have tightened inspections. All units shipped from the plant pass a very thorough inspection. But nothing seems to have slowed the complaints and the canceled orders.

You put down the reports with a sigh. The problem with the Beker-9, if unchecked, could destroy the high-quality image you've worked for decades to build. Beker's reputation for quality is what has allowed it to compete successfully against much larger firms that produce similar products. At worst, Beker's very existence could be threatened.

As president, you were very involved in the introduction of the Beker-9 and have an emotional stake in its success. In addition, because the telecommunication industry in general and the pager market in particular are among the fastest-growing sectors of the U.S. economy, there's an enormous financial pressure to quickly fix this problem.

Leaders live in a constant tug-of-war with cause and effect. When the effects build up to where they require action, the leader has to get working on finding the root cause.

It's sometimes easy to recognize the big effect, say, a broken turbine, high attrition, or soaring health care costs. But, as in the Beker case, it's the complex problem—maybe originating from more than one source and often cumulative in its effects—that's most troubling. Remember the old story about the frog's reaction to heat? When he's put into a beaker of boiling water, he leaps out. But when he's placed in cool water and the temperature is slowly increased, he sits there or swims around until he's boiled.

It's often this way in life. At Beker, for example, the pager problem isn't yet a live-or-die problem, but it soon could be. The defects haven't shut the company down or even stopped pager production. You haven't been sued. You're not about to be fired. You're not going bankrupt—yet.

But the rate of defects is unacceptable and growing. And the cause is opaque. It could spring from faulty parts, careless subcontractors, poor engineering, or some combination of those or other causes. Who knows?

In real life, the toughest problems are often just like that. They can creep up on us from several different angles. That's where Cause Analysis comes in. It helps us to detect the real causes, saving us from wasteful trial and error.

You get your team assembled, and you waste no time.

Let's get this meeting going. First, I'd like a progress report from the Sales Manager.

"This thing's driving us nuts," he says. "Fielding all these complaints is a nightmare. Lack of confidence in the Beker-9 is growing, not only among the customers, but among the salespeople, too. They're getting flak from many of their biggest accounts. Morale's not good, and a couple of my best people are already talking about quitting."

You got any ideas?

"Well, one of the guys in Medical Sales says his customers haven't had much of a problem with the B-9. He attributes that to his product training—he's gotten pretty good at showing the doctors and nurses how to use the pager properly. So I sent him down to the copper mine in Arizona, where they've had a lot of defective pagers. I thought it might help, but it didn't. To make it worse, his trip ruffled the feathers of the Industrial Sales manager. Since then, the mining company has canceled a big order of Beker-9s, and the Industrial Sales manager blames it on my 'interference with his customer.' I'm at my wit's end. I don't know what to do."

Uh oh! Not good.

A leader's worst—but not uncommon—response is: "I *think* I know the cause, and therefore, I will take an action." That satisfies a certain primal urge, but too often such hunches lead to wasted energy and resources.

It's like having an inexperienced mechanic fix your car. He may start at the fan belt and work back, changing parts along the way. Eventually he solves the problem, but only after a long time and at great injury to your wallet.

And in life, unlike the relative simplicity of a gasoline engine, such actions can muddy the situation and make it more difficult to resolve. At Beker, you now see that you've not only got a demoralized sales force, but also political warfare between two of your sales departments.

Let's hear from Quality Control.

"We've tightened inspection specifications, both on incoming vendors and on outgoing assembled units. This has made us very unpopular with our suppliers and, in fact, with our own people in Manufacturing.

"Nothing seems to help. So we sent a couple inspectors out to our second-source suppliers of wire and resistors. That's a highly unusual step, but we can't be too careful on this one."

What did they find out?

"One of our prime suppliers has experienced a series of small chemical fires. They think it might be some sort of industrial sabotage."

What's that have to do with Beker-9?

"We don't know. Maybe something, maybe nothing."

This Quality Control guy sounds like he's taking shots in the dark.

That's another instinctual error. Leaders often think, if I poke around in enough dark corners, maybe I'll find something. If I fix enough things, maybe I'll remove the cause.

Too often, though, they fix things that aren't broken. That's time-consuming and expensive, both in terms of money and human relations. And it may end up causing other problems, too. If any problem is worth fixing, it deserves a logical, analytical approach that minimizes dead ends and points to a single action.

In Cause Analysis, it's useful to think of the problem as an iceberg. What you can see only hints at the entire problem. But, while you want to see the whole iceberg, you don't want to have to explore the whole polar ice cap to do so.

O.K., let's have a report from vice president, Marketing/Public Relations.

"We recommend the company cease producing the Beker-9, recall all existing Beker-9s, and replace them with the earlier Beker-7 model. It's bulkier, weighs more, and doesn't have the calculator, which many of our customers like, but it's more reliable."

That's pretty radical, isn't it?

"Yes, but it's a radical problem. It's better to bite the bullet now than allow our market share to deteriorate. It's like amputating a gangrenous limb. We can explain it to our customers by honestly saying it's for their benefit. And we can hold out the hope that production of the Beker-9 will be resumed when all this is taken care of. It's tough medicine, but we'll be better off for it in the long run."

It's a strong stance. But will it really help solve the problem?

One of the most common mistakes leaders make is confusing symptoms, causes, and effects. Here are some definitions:

Symptoms
The visible parts of the problem.
Causes
Verifiable stimuli that make something happen, that create the effects.
Effects
The impact of the problem. Symptoms are part of the effects.

Symptoms reveal the problem, but they don't explain it. They're just clues. Sometimes they require action. But the good leader doesn't delude himself or herself into thinking that action on the symptoms will remove the problem. The cause still needs to be located and fixed.

An example: On my college football team, a friend named Mike, who played tight end, showed up at training camp about 15 pounds overweight. That wasn't so bad—we all wanted to be heavier in those days—but he began dropping passes, a lot of passes.

When the coach asked him why, he said, "I can't see as well as I used to. Everything's a little fuzzy." Rather than benching Mike, the coach sent him to the team doctor, who referred him to an eye specialist. It seemed obvious to everyone that Mike needed glasses.

Get some contact lenses—we all thought—and the problem would be solved.

But as the eye doctor gave Mike an exam, he noticed that the blood vessels in Mike's eyes were unusually large. Rather than fit him with glasses, he sent Mike to a general practitioner. The general practitioner gave Mike a full physical and asked him questions such as, "Has your diet changed in the last six months?"

Mike said he'd recently married an Italian-American woman who cooked pasta almost every day. Which was great, Mike added, because, for one thing, it was marvelous pasta and, secondly, he'd hurt a tooth in the last game of the previous year and couldn't chew anything hard anyway. He thought the tooth would heal itself as he was told by a friend, but it still bothered him.

The doctor's diagnosis: A dietary imbalance was causing the swelling of the blood vessels, which in turn was fogging Mike's vision, which in turn led to the dropped passes. The doctor's prescription: Forget about eyeglasses, but get the tooth fixed and start eating more protein and less pasta.

Mike did. As a result, he lost the 15 pounds in a few weeks, got his normal vision back—and stopped dropping passes. He had a great senior year in football.

The moral of the story: It ended happily because no one treated just the symptoms. They kept investigating. The coach didn't demote Mike just because he dropped passes. The eye doctor didn't prescribe glasses just because Mike's vision was fuzzy. The general practitioner didn't treat just the weight problem, but instead asked enough process questions to find out what really had changed. And the true root cause turned out to be a surprise to all of us!

This process is called "stair stepping." It requires the discipline to keep asking questions and to refrain from taking action until you've arrived at the *true root cause*.

The symptom at Beker is that customers are sending back their pagers or canceling orders. You can continue to send out hundreds of replacement pagers. You can try to get your salespeople to sell more pagers. Or, as the Marketing/PR person suggests, you can quit producing the Beker-9 pager.

All of these actions deal just with the symptom. They may be good short-term actions while you try to get to the bottom of things. But, obviously, if you haven't figured out why the pagers go kaput, you're just buying time. And in business, time is definitely money!

Engineering, what's your take on all this?

"Normally, we have a less than 1 percent defect rate. Now it's 20 percent. We don't know why. We redesigned the housing and the circuitry when we upgraded the Beker-7 model to the Beker-9. The 9 has got the new, unsealed slide switch that customers like because it's easier to use."

Should we halt production?

"Your call. It's doable, if that's the decision. It'd take us about 45 days to turn around our assembly line and start making the Beker-7s again."

Forty-five days without a product while the rejects and cancellations flood in!

Let's see, who haven't we heard from yet? Oh, Director of R&D. Go ahead.

"Well, sir, as you can imagine, we've spent a lot of time looking at this, using the most stringent tests. Down in my shop, we all have our pet theories."

Such as?

"One guy thinks it's the switch. Another points to our method of soldering. Or the kind of solder we use. Or the kind of soldering guns."

And?

"And there's been some slight improvement as we tinker with those things, but not much. None of the theories really prove out so far."

Any other ideas?

"Examination of the returned pagers shows that many of the parts around the switch have cracked, broken, or stripped insulation. The only way we've been able to duplicate that effect in the lab is by subjecting these parts to abnormal heat, cold, or tempera-

ture fluctuations. By 'abnormal,' I mean, really extreme temperatures—far above or below what's likely to be experienced in any
user's environment."

So, where could these temperature extremes occur?

"I honestly don't know. We've gone over our manufacturing
process with a fine-tooth comb. We can't find a source of such
variances."

Hhhmmm! Interesting. But maddeningly inconclusive.

You dismiss the meeting, telling your people to change nothing
until you personally can digest the facts.

They all file out your office, leaving you feeling as if you're a
physician with a patient who's got a mysterious, life-threatening
illness. In fact, now that you think about it, that's a good analogy.
Doctors deal with Cause Analysis all the time. They call it
diagnosis. When you go to the doctor, he or she asks questions:

- What's wrong?
- What were you doing when you noticed the pain?
- When did it start?
- How frequent is the pain?
- How severe is it?
- Is it getting worse?

The Cause Analysis Process

STEP ONE

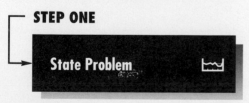

Similarly, in Cause Analysis, you collect relevant data, step-by-
step. The first step is describing the problem, including its location,
timing, and magnitude.

In the Beker-9 situation, we can already state the problem in a
general sense, much as a patient might describe his or her ailment to
the doctor. In essence, *Beker's customers are reporting an unacceptable
number of defective Beker-9 pagers, especially in field operations*. The
trend began nine months ago, soon after the unit's introduction, and

continues to rise. The problem not only imperils the Beker-9 line, but threatens to undermine the company's reputation and morale.

STEP TWO

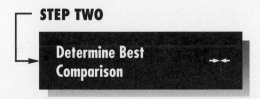

Determine Best Comparison

The doctor, though, wouldn't stop there. He or she would ask questions to get at essential facts not yet revealed. Medical diagnosis, like Cause Analysis, is a process of comparison. You can't just describe what happened. The doctor and the leader both need to ask questions that will yield valid, precise, comparative data.

So to get at the root cause of the problem, you'll need to list in more detail the answers to What, Where, When, and Magnitude questions. I recommend you prepare a Cause Analysis work sheet.

It would look something like this:

Problem Description	*Observed Facts* Identify what you know about the problem as specifically as possible.
What What is wrong?	Many Beker-9s receive intermittently then fail completely.
Where Where is the object located when the problem is observed?	In the field: construction site, grainery, mine, etc.
Where does the defect appear on the object?	Switch housing
When When was the defect first seen?	Just after introduction 9 months ago
Magnitude How many are defective? What is the trend?	20% Increasing

This work sheet clarifies the description. You've clearly set down the facts about the present situation. However, just as you did with the Mexican lunch, you now need a comparison. You must look at an earlier set of facts in order to figure out what's changed. Making such a comparison can be arduous and some leaders resist generating parallel facts. But usually that's the only way to get to the core of the problem.

In this case, you can compare the Beker-9 with its predecessor, the Beker-7 pager, using the same set of questions. You can compare the field locations that report the problem to those that don't, and you can compare the Beker-9 when it didn't have a problem to when it did.

Add these parallel facts to your work sheet:

Problem Description	*Observed Facts* Identify what you know about the problem as specifically as possible.	*Comparative Facts* Reasonable and logical comparisons: things that are most similar to, but not the same as, the Observed Fact.
What What is wrong?	Many Beker-9s receive intermittently then fail completely.	Beker-7s
Where Where is the object located when the problem is observed? Where does the defect appear on the object?	In the field: construction site, grainery, mine, etc. Switch housing	Cola plant, hospital Case, speaker
When When was the defect first seen?	Just after introduction 9 months ago	Prior to introduction
Magnitude How many are defective? What is the trend?	20% Increasing	Less than 1% Constant

Now you've set up clear comparisons in the What, Where, When, and Magnitude descriptions of the problem by using paired sets of facts. That's always the framework for discovering cause.

That's how you solved the riddle of the Mexican lunch, for example. It's also how the doctor diagnoses your ailment. He or she compares your signs and symptoms against those learned in medical school, those of other patients, or those from when you were well. He or she will also try to pinpoint the exact time you first started noticing the pain to determine what has changed. By finding what you did differently at the time you first began feeling ill, the doctor can usually determine what caused your illness.

STEP THREE

Identify Clues

Having two sets of facts isn't enough in itself. Common sense tells us we must isolate the differences and changes—clues—that might account for the problem. This is fundamental to all problem solving.

Logically, the first crucial question becomes What's different about Observed Facts versus Comparative Facts? This is important because the answer will become your test basis for likely causes.

Comparative Facts	*Clues* 🔎	
Reasonable and logical comparisons: things that are most similar to, but not the same as, the Observed Fact.	*Differences*	*Changes*
Beker-7s	Beker-9—new unsealed slide switch, lighter housing, added calculator.	
Cola plant, hospital Case, speaker	User's environment has dust, debris, greater temp. variances.	
Prior to introduction	Beker-9 actually in use.	
Less than 1% Constant	No difference facts known. No difference facts known.	

Issac Newton found that a body in motion tends to continue moving in the same direction unless and until acted upon by an outside force. In other words, something has to change to give us different results—more clues!

So what has happened in the transition from the Beker-7 to Beker-9 product lines? Let's list changes relevant to the Differences:

Comparative Facts ◄ Reasonable and logical comparisons: things that are most similar to, but not the same as, the Observed Fact.	**Clues** 🔍 Differences	Changes
Beker-7s	Beker-9—new unsealed slide switch, lighter housing, added calculator.	No relevant changes.
Cola plant, hospital Case, speaker	User's environment has dust, debris, greater temp. variances.	No relevant changes.
Prior to introduction	Beker-9 actually in use.	Taken out of testing and introduced to market.
Less than 1% Constant	No difference facts known. No difference facts known.	No relevant changes. No relevant changes.

Hhhmmm! Now you're beginning to get some ideas about cause. There's something different about the new switch as well as something different about where the Beker-9 is being used.

You're ready to make some informed predictions about cause. That naturally leads you to the next step.

STEP FOUR

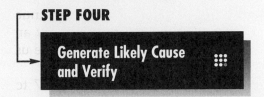

Generate Likely Cause
and Verify

Those clues you uncovered in Step Three now can be used to help you develop a theory. Think back to your meeting with your department heads.

The R&D director said many of the defective pagers have cracked, broken, or stripped insulation around the switches. And many of those returned pagers were used in mines and mills where there's dust and other contaminants.

One of the main differences between the Beker 9 and the Beker 7 is that the Beker 9 has a new, unsealed slide switch. The Beker 7, which had been sold to similar customers as the Beker 9 but had a sealed slide switch, hadn't experienced the difficulties the Beker 9 is now experiencing in dirty environments.

Following this line, the Beker 9 isn't experiencing difficulties in cleaner, mostly indoor environments. This would account for the failed attempt by the Sales Manager to train the Beker 9 users in the Arizona copper mine.

R&D ruled out the possibly of temperatures causing the problem when they determined that only extreme temperatures above or below that which would be experienced at a customer's site could account for the damaged interior of the Beker 9.

The chemical fires at one of your suppliers couldn't be the cause because then you would see the problem with all of your customers, not just the ones in dirtier environments.

Quality Control's increased inspection of the Beker 9 before, during, and after its production could not find a cause to the problem because, at those points, the Beker 9 hadn't yet been exposed to the dirty environments where the problem manifests itself.

So...the Beker 9 seems to malfunction because of dust and other contaminants getting through the unsealed slide switch which eventually damages the Beker 9 to the point where it can only receive intermittent reception and then fails completely.

You get the vice president of Engineering on the phone and tell him to reconstruct the slide switch on the Beker 9.

Then you call Quality Control.

"Two things I need you to do. First, contact Engineering, get a sample of the new switch which will be used on the Beker 9. Then simulate conditions that would be found at some of our "dirtier" client's facilities," you tell them.

"And?"

"And see if contaminants are still entering into the pager. If they are, get that pager to the point where it will be fully protected."

The Quality Control manager says he'll get on it right away. But then he adds, "How did you figure all this out so quickly?"

"Elementary, my dear Watson!" you reply with a chuckle before giving him a short lesson in Cause Analysis. "Let's say, for instance, you and I had a Mexican lunch and..."

You don't know for sure that you've found the cause of the Beker-9 problem until the tests are in. But it looks very promising.

You're certainly glad you took the time and made the effort to use Cause Analysis instead of reacting quickly, perhaps emotionally. If improving the packaging is the key, that will certainly be a shorter, less expensive option than curtailing production of this popular, useful product. By using one of the thinking skills, you also avoided having this crisis become more political, with warring departments blaming one another and trying to wiggle out of responsibility.

All in all, you say to yourself, *good show!* You took an hour or so and solved a costly problem that many companies might have wrestled fruitlessly with for months. You're justly proud of yourself, even though anyone could have done what you did by applying common sense. But only *if* they knew the process, *if* they knew not just the facts, ma'am, but also how to analyze them.

Realistic and True

The Beker case is not only realistic, it's true. A major electronics firm had just such a problem, went through just such a Cause Analysis, and by the firm's own estimate, saved some $25 million by quickly getting at the root of the problem in a short time instead of tearing off in a dozen different directions with uncertain results.

That's a dramatic example of the awesome power of a little Cause Analysis detective work. But not just complex corporate problems can be solved by Cause Analysis.

Just for fun, imagine a simpler, more personal example: Let's say a bunch of trees near your summer cabin are dying.

You first noticed them last spring but didn't pay too much attention. This year, the problem seems to be getting worse, and you and your family are worried. This lovely, leafy retreat has been in your family for generations. You've got the stop these trees from dying—but first you've got to figure out *why* they're dying.

At a family picnic under some of those very trees, everybody seems to have a theory. Your brother says it's probably some kind of insect, so you should climb up in the tops of the trees and inspect for bugs. Somebody else, fearing you might break your leg, suggests instead that you hire an entomologist, or better yet, pay a pest-control firm to spray with insecticide.

Your sister doesn't like the idea of using chemicals. She says maybe the trees are just old and ought to be cut down and replaced with saplings. It will be a long time before the new trees provide much beauty or shade, but at least that would be better than just watching the old ones wither away.

Your sister-in-law says a better plan would be, for starters, to get a forester, or some other tree expert, to learn if the dying ones are all the same species. Or, somebody else suggests, maybe the problem is something in the soil, in which case, you need an agronomist, not an entomologist or a forester.

The possibilities are many. And time-consuming. And probably expensive. Instead, you decide to do a Cause Analysis.

First, you *describe the problem:* Some, but not all, of the trees around the cabin are dying.

Next, instead of hiring experts to tell you if bugs, diseases, or age is killing the trees, you decide to *set down the observed facts versus the comparative facts.*

Observed Facts	**Comparative Facts**
Identify what you know about the problem as specifically as possible.	Reasonable and logical comparisons: things that are most similar to, but not the same as, the Observed Fact.
What	
Some trees are dying	Most of the trees aren't dying
Where	
The trees next to the stream	The trees not near the stream
When	
Began dying last Spring	Not before last Spring
Magnitude	
Trend increasing	Remaining the same

Next, you determine *the relevant differences between the observed and comparative facts.* The dying trees began to be affected last spring, and they're all near the stream. Trees not near the stream are doing fine, and all the trees were healthy until last spring.

Next you determine *what has changed to cause the problem.* You remember a new, small manufacturing plant that was built a mile or so up the road a year or so ago. It's upstream, and the time frame fits.

Next, *you generate a likely cause.* Something's in the water that wasn't there before last spring, and it's affecting those trees nearest the stream.

Next, you *test this likely cause.* You go and look at the trees upstream from the small factory. They're fine. Then you check out the trees downstream from the plant but upstream from your place. Lots of them are dying along either side of the stream.

Finally, you *verify this cause.* You can have the water tested. Or you can go to environmental authorities with your likely cause, or perhaps even to the plant manager.

The ultimate verification will be curtailing the effluent, or lessening its toxicity, then watching to see if the trees recover or at least cease dying.

Delaying Guesswork

So, by using a method that was less disruptive, expensive, and time-consuming, you came up with the root cause. You didn't have to risk your neck climbing to the tops of the trees; you didn't have to spray poison or hire an expert or cut down trees that perhaps will recover.

Instead, you took the extra—but vital—steps of listing the comparative facts, figuring out the relevant differences and coming up with the key change. You eliminated the guesswork.

The time you lost in taking a disciplined approach was more than made up by quickly getting to the solution a step or so later. If you had just responded to the symptoms—sprayed, or cut the trees or hired experts—you not only would have wasted time and money, but you might have made the situation worse. While you flailed about blindly, the pollution would have continued, perhaps causing more trees to die.

Becoming a Better Detective

Remember, the facts are only as important as your ability to use them. For example, Cause Analysis, though it's never described as such on your favorite TV crime show, is really the skill that detectives employ. I've taught the thinking skills at several police departments; the key for the police, is to find the *differences and changes*.

In the cops' case, the difference is, who has a motive for murder. First, they would list the possible suspects on a Cause Analysis work sheet, just as you or I would list the differences in our business or family situation.

Then they'd try to identify changes relative to the suspects' relationship to the victim. Did Suspect A stand to inherit a lot of money if the victim died? Was Suspect B likely to triumph romantically if the victim were out of the way? Was suspect C being treated differently because of financial problems? And so forth.

Your situation and that faced by the homicide investigator may be radically different, but the process is parallel. And being a better "detective" is a big advantage for any modern leader.

Now What Do You Do?

Okay, we've learned how to find the true root cause of the problem. So what do we do now? *Fix* it, right? Not necessarily. We may find that approach too costly or inconvenient.

Actually, you have three choices of *action* once you've found the root cause:

- **Interim**. Doing something temporary that will buy you time to permanently solve the problem when it's more convenient or less costly.

- **Adaptive**. Deciding to live with the problem because it's more expensive or time-consuming to fix it than to endure it.

- **Corrective**. Fixing or eliminating the problem by addressing the true root cause.

For example, not long ago on a very stormy January evening, I was having a dinner party at my home. Everything was going fine until, suddenly, the ceiling started leaking because of all the rain.

I didn't want to disrupt the party, but I didn't want to flood the house, either. Basically, I had these choices:

- **Interim**. Put a bucket under the leak and fix the roof later.

- **Adaptive**. Decide not to fix the roof. (I'd save money and could deal with the occasional big storm by just keeping the bucket handy.)

- **Corrective**. Call the roofer and get someone up there to fix the leak permanently.

Once we've done our Cause Analysis, we're all confronted with these kinds of choices. The Adaptive or Interim actions can be quite tempting. They usually cost less in time, money, and effort and may give a temporary sense of relief.

But often they're bad leadership. For example, if I had taken the Adaptive action with my roof, sooner or later—maybe when that next big storm hit or certainly when I went to sell my house—there would be a reckoning, and perhaps a more costly one, with the leaky roof. Or if I chose the Interim solution, there's a chance—

perhaps a likelihood—that once the sun came out and the dripping stopped, I'd be diverted to other tasks and wouldn't even think about the roof until there was another rainstorm.

In any event, with my leaky roof, the true root cause wasn't as hard to figure out as it was in the case of the Beker-9s, the dying trees, or even the Mexican lunch. But in each case, we would then need to decide what our action was going to be: Interim, Adaptive, or Corrective.

There may be times when each is appropriate. But as proactive thinkers and leaders, we should be biased toward the Corrective solution. A problem deferred is not a problem solved.

Chapter **Three**

Skill 3 Decision Making
What Action to Take Now

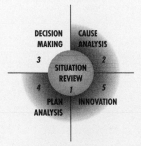

A geophysics company on the Gulf Coast had a wonderful problem: A spectacularly good year had brought in so much cash the firm didn't know what to do with it all.

Company executives debated how to manage the windfall. They would need the money for expansion in a couple years. Meanwhile, they wanted to invest the cash and try to build up the surplus. But invest in *what?*

They discussed buying various kinds of negotiable securities. But that didn't seem very aggressive or very exciting. They thought about acquiring other companies, but that was too bold, too risky. They considered buying some land, but that was too long-term.

"Shrimp!" somebody then suggested. That was it! Suddenly excited by the prospects of doubling their money and having perhaps an unlimited corporate supply of gumbo, the executives quickly made plans to buy a fleet of shrimp boats.

They knew shrimping could be quite profitable. What's more, they were proud of the tradition, a regional trade that couldn't be practiced in, say, Iowa or Montana. So the geophysics executives started to look into acquiring, outfitting, and operating shrimp boats. They began hunting for excess freezer capacity, and they drew up contracts for harvesting and marketing.

Reviewing the Purpose

But then the company president wisely halted the effort long enough to ask the Decision Making questions, one of which is *What is the purpose of the decision*?

The purpose was to make money from surplus cash over the next 24 months. But in the heat of the moment, that had somehow gotten twisted into "Get into the shrimp boat business."

As a result of asking the right series of questions, the firm decided instead to just buy the shrimp from the big shrimping firms and market it in other parts of the country. Because its involvement was to be so short-term, the firm wisely avoided tying up a lot of capital in boats, crews, and equipment. As a result, it ended up making a lot more money on its surplus cash.

Cause Analysis, which we looked at in the last chapter, deals with analyzing past events, finding the reason for what's already happened. But Decision Making involves making a choice about what to do now.

That choice may take different forms. It can involve a decision among several alternatives, such as the would-be shrimpers faced. Or it can just be a choice between a yes or no, thumbs up or thumbs down. Or it can involve deciding among almost countless alternatives, such as who, among all the hundreds of applicants, should be hired as a receptionist.

Whichever the case, you need to learn to ask these questions:

- What is the purpose of the decision?
- Is a decision really necessary now?
- What are the selection criteria?
- What alternatives should you consider?
- What are the risks?
- How serious are those risks?

Decisiveness versus Decision Making

Almost everything we do in life is a result of the decisions we make or fail to make. Decision Making, then, may be our most important thinking skill. And, in practice, it should be the highest form of the art. But too often it's not.

Instead, when faced with a knotty situation, the tendency is to want to go on the attack—make a quick decision and put it all behind you. Sell the troubled division, fire the poor performer, hire a new consultant or subcontractor…do *something!*

In many organizations, managers are rewarded for making snap judgments like that. Uncertainty is equated with weakness. But often a very "decisive" person is a very poor decision maker. Decisions that are made without studying the facts rarely turn out well. Instead, the best decision maker is not the one who makes the *quickest* choice, but the one who makes the *best* choice after doing a thorough analysis.

Angela is assistant customer service manager at Metropolitan Medical, a New York City-based national distributor of medical supplies. Business is good, and the company president decides it's time to open a customer service department in the Midwest. "Angela, I want you to go to Chicago—one of my favorite cities, incidentally; I *love* the restaurants, the nightlife, the energy of the place—and lease us an office."

"Great!"

"Better yet, I want you to head up that office. It's a nice step up for you, a good job in an exciting place. And if you do well, who knows what could be next for you?"

"Thanks, Mr. Harris. I'm sure I'll justify your confidence. When do you want this up and running?"

"Soon," he says, "But, first, let me show you something." He opens a folder listing his standards for the new office. "You'll want to talk to others also, and you may have some ideas of your own about this new office. But do your best to see that the criteria I've listed here are met. Also, if it's possible to get a place near Lake Michigan, one that has a bit of Chicago character, that'd be terrific!"

He gives Angela the folder and sends her on her way. This is the most responsibility she's ever been given. "For sure," she thinks, "I've go to do this right!"

The Standard Process

Angela faces one of the most common forms of Decision Making: a choice between limited alternatives, in this case, where to locate the new office. Angela wants to make sure she's objective about the sites and that her range of alternatives cover all essential criteria.

She'll want to be careful not to preselect a "pet" alternative. She's a little worried about Mr. Harris's knowledge of the area and what may be his emotional investment in certain sites. But, Angela thinks, "I'll cross that bridge when I come to it."

Cause Analysis, you'll recall from the last chapter, is a deductive process. The leader gathers facts, then narrows them down to a single cause or set of causes. In Decision Making, though, the leader keeps building up the database until it can be used to screen out less desirable alternatives.

There's uncertainty to be dealt with in both cases, but it differs vastly. In Cause Analysis, the uncertainty is what has already occurred. So the manager looks at past events and narrows the search to where he or she can confidently decide how to address the problem. Then the manager verifies that he or she identified the right cause.

But in Decision Making, the uncertainty is now. The manager compares the relative impact of alternatives without ever knowing for sure what might have happened if he or she had chosen another one. By its very nature this can be a difficult process. But here are the basic steps to effective Decision Making:

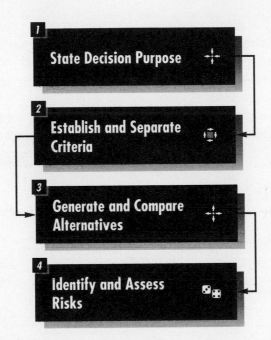

┌─ **STEP ONE**
│
└──▶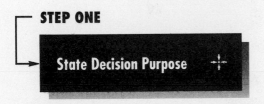

Before jumping head-first into a sea of choices, you must ask some questions, such as, *what* are you deciding—and *why*.

This helps in shaping alternatives and keeps you from getting too far afield, as the would-be shrimp magnates did before reining themselves in.

It's always tempting to skip this step. Knowing that some action is being taken can be comforting. But acting before analyzing only creates an illusion that you're on top of the problem. You need to question the purpose by asking three questions:

- *What choice am I trying to make?* If a regional sales manager, for example, resigns, the quick, obvious question might be How do I replace her? But maybe the questions should be

Do I need to replace her? Could someone else absorb that task? Should I merge the regional sales function with some other function? These queries should be your starting points.

- *Why is this decision necessary?* Let's say the decision is to buy a new copying machine because the old one doesn't work well. But you should ask Is leasing is a better option? or How about getting a better maintenance contract on the old copier? You need to make sure the decision resolves your concern.

- *What was the last decision made?* Each decision should fit somewhere on the chain of logic. For example, perhaps the decision purpose is "To select a training program for implementation of the job-enrichment program." But was it really decided that "job enrichment" would solve our morale problem? And, if so, is a training program what's needed to enrich jobs? Good analysis here will keep you from adding two and two and getting three.

In Angela's case, the choice she's faced with is finding a Chicago office site to lease. It's necessary because the company wants to expand its customer service to the Midwest, and this choice follows Mr. Harris's desire for such an office to be located in Chicago.

Pretty simple for Angela. But the next step gets tougher.

STEP TWO

Establish and Separate Criteria

Okay, so now you know that what you're deciding is important and that the decision follows logically in the chain of decisions. Now you begin the actual process of choosing.

Good decisions are those that get the required results. You must figure out what you want those required results to be. They become your Decision Criteria, and they're the basis on which your choice will be made.

The first thing you've got to find out is what you want to achieve. This step is also helpful in a group situation because it ensures that everybody who's affected by the decision gets to specify their needs.

Angela takes a look at Mr. Harris's list of criteria. First, he wants the office to open within three months under a long-term lease that won't cost more than $250,000 rent in the first year and won't increase by more than 10 percent a year. Second, because he's so fond of the city, he'd like the office to be in a building having what he calls "a bit of Chicago character," preferably on or near the lake.

Then Angela talks to other employees. Those who will work there stress the importance of being within walking distance of several good restaurants. The salespeople, who will be driving to meet their clients, want a large parking area near the office.

The firm's support staff tells her that for the planned number of employees, their furniture, and storage, she'll need a minimum of 8,000 square feet. Angela, being a frugal manager and not wanting to attract unseemly attention to the cost of her maiden start-up in a glamorous city, adds another criterion of her own: the lowest rent possible.

"Whew!" Angela sighs. In Chicago, where parking is scarce and rents are high, this all is going to be a big order.

But, at least, Angela now has a list of criteria:

Criteria

✓ Minimum 8,000 square feet
✓ Available in 3 months
✓ Maximum rent $250,000 first year
✓ Long-term lease
✓ Maximum 10% annual rent increase
✓ Nearby parking
✓ Close to restaurants
✓ Chicago lakefront "character"
✓ Reasonably low rent

Reviewing her list, Angela discovers a key characteristic of decision criteria: Some of these are absolute requirements (Limits); others would be things she wants to have in her ultimate decision but may be able to live without (Desirables). The two are distinguished below:

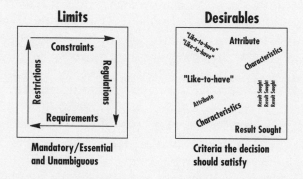

If a place lacked significant Windy City "character," for example, or the restaurants were more than a short walk away, she still might be able to sell it to Mr. Harris if most of the other needs were met. But if it cost more than his $250,000 upper limit—*no way!*

So she must decide which criteria are Limits and which are Desirables.

Angela first separates the Limits from her decision criteria list:

Criteria

✓	Minimum 8,000 square feet
	~~Available in 2 months~~

Limits ("must haves")

✓	Minimum 8,000 square feet
✓	Maximum rent $250,000 first year
✓	Maximum 10% annual rent increase

Angela has no wiggle room on the these. Mr. Harris made it abundantly clear that his feet are in concrete on the rent and any rent increases. And the administration people convinced her that anything less than 8,000 feet just wouldn't work.

But what about the rest of the criteria? Are some of the Desirables more desirable than others? Of course. Every manager knows life is a series of trade-offs. So what Angela needs to do is rank the Desirables so that when trade-off time arrives, she'll get the best deal for the most people at the lowest cost.

We all make trade-offs every day: when, placing a higher priority on speed than price, we send a package by private courier; when we defer maintenance on machinery to keep short-run production high; when we hire the more experienced, higher-salaried candidates because they bring a needed skill we can't get from a novice. Thus, Angela needs to rank the Desirables in case she has to jettison some of them during her search and negotiation.

Quantify the Desirables

The simplest way to rank the Desirables is to assign each a number. The highest-rated criterion would be given a "10." Each of the other Desirables is then compared to that "10" and ranked based on its relative value and impact.

How do you make these rankings? By thinking about them and, importantly, asking others what they think.

Angela knows Mr. Harris is anxious to get this new operation up and moving. So she assigns the highest priority to the space being available in three months. Then she ranks the others in relation to that. Her Desirables list ends up looking like so:

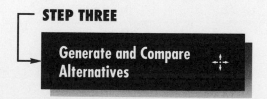

Criteria

✓ Minimum 8,000 square feet	
✓ Available in 3 months	

Desirables ("want to haves")

	Value
✓ Available in 3 months	10
✓ Long-term lease	6
✓ Nearby parking	9
✓ Close to restaurants	5
✓ Chicago lakefront "character"	3
✓ Reasonably low rent	4

She'd still like to get a cheap place and with Mr. Harris's much-vaunted Chicago "character." But she figures that if she meets most, or all, of the other criteria—including parking for the salespeople and restaurants for general morale purposes—she could hedge a little on the office's price and the ambiance.

Now she's feeling better. She feels sure that she now knows what's involved and how those elements stack up against one another. What she lacks are possible sites.

STEP THREE

Generate and Compare Alternatives

Looking at commercial real estate near downtown Chicago, Angela found, is not a task for the faint of heart. But having figured out the criteria, Angela could gather her data purposefully. Her search became a planned process rather than a reaction to information as it surfaced.

It was helpful to be able to tell her real estate agent exactly what she was looking for. That narrowed the choices and saved some time. The agent first showed her a site near Lake Shore Drive that was ideal—dripping with Chicago "character"—but way beyond Mr. Harris's maximum rent. Then Angela looked at places that were within the price guidelines, but where none would feel safe walking to lunch or even parking their car.

Fortunately, the agent had some other possibilities. There was a spot on Michigan Avenue just north of the Loop. The 9,000-square-foot site rented for $250,000 a year, pushing right up against Mr. Harris's limit. A five-year lease was available, with an annual rent increase of 6 percent.

Parking wasn't the best, but the restaurants certainly were. And the eastward-facing office had a wonderful view of the lake. You sure would know you weren't in Omaha.

Angela looked at another spot in a popular warehouse district on Grand Avenue. The brick building was a little bigger (10,000 square feet) and cheaper ($180,500 a year) but it was being refurbished and might not be available within 90 days. It had lots of parking, but a hot dog kiosk in the next block was the closest approximation to a neighborhood restaurant. It had a rent increase of 7 percent per year.

Then she looked at a La Salle Street site. It was the smallest (8,000 square feet) of the three and also the priciest ($300,000 a year) because it was near the heart of the financial district. It had a rent increase of 10 percent per year.

Angela was torn. They all had their plusses. She wished she could combine parts of each. But that isn't the way life works and leaders rarely have that luxury. What leaders *do* have is the power of analysis.

So Angela knew she needed to make some tough comparisons. But comparing what to what?

Here's the fundamental principle: Always compare the alternatives (in this case, the sites) back to the criteria, *not to each other.* Never compare a solution to a solution. To do so is to fall prey to "solution blindness"; pursuing alternatives while having lost sight of the goal. That's a recipe for buyer's remorse. ("It seemed like a good idea at the time," is an all-too-frequent refrain.)

Another common pitfall at this stage is "paralysis by over-analysis." That's when gathering data about alternatives becomes an end in itself. It's almost an axiom of American life that decisions often aren't made until most of the good options are gone. Such procrastination just makes the decision even more difficult.

So it's important to understand that good Decision Making
means making *the best choice with the facts then available.* You'll never
have every possible fact, and all the available facts won't be positive. The cure for both these ills is to make sure you relate alternatives to the criteria. This forces you to focus on key information.

So what must Angela do?

Well, first she double-checks that her Limits—her absolute min-
imums—are still valid. Limits are usually created in the early stages
of the Decision Making process, and sometimes they're overtaken
by events. For example, if when she arrived in Chicago to begin her
search, she had found that there were no offices available below
$250,000 a year, that would have made her criteria invalid.

But the Limits are workable. So, she compares each of the office
site alternatives to her Limits to see how they stack up. At this
point, the alternatives either pass or fail Angela's Limits "filter" for
further consideration: Each is either a "go" or a "no-go."

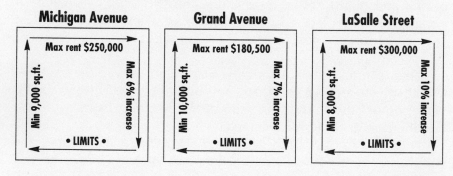

Both the Michigan Avenue and the Grand Avenue sites meet
those requirements. The La Salle Street space, however, does not.
It's too pricey; Mr. Harris will never go for it. Angela scratches it
off the list.

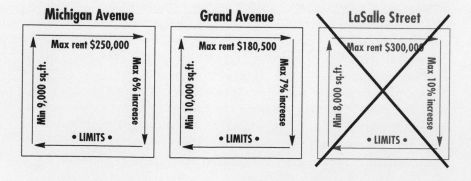

That leaves her with two sites conforming to the Limits. She must now score the sites on the Desirables. She does that by asking the question: "Which alternative best meets that criterion?"

On the "available within 3 months" criterion, the best alternative—Michigan Avenue—receives a 10. The Grand Avenue site receives a score based on its strength compared to the criterion. So it gets an 8 because availability, while probable, is a bit less clear there.

Alternatives		A. Michigan Ave.			B. Grand Ave.		
Desirables	*Values*	*Desirables*	*Score*	*Wt. Score*		*Score*	*Wt. Score*
Available in 3 months	10	Definitely	10		Probably	8	
Long-term lease	6						
Nearby parking	9						
Close to restaurants	5						
Chicago "lakefront" character	3						
Reasonably low rent	4						
			Total			Total	

And so on. For each Desirable, Angela judges how each site measures up. What results is a profile of how each site measures up against all criteria.

To get a total picture, she would simply multiply the value of each of the Desirables against the relative score of the sites. For example, the criterion of availability has a value of 10. Multiplying that times the Michigan Avenue site's availability score of 10 yields a weighted score of 100; the Grand Avenue site's availability score of 8 equals a weighted score of 80 (see below).

Alternatives		A. Michigan Ave.			B. Grand Ave.		
Desirables	*Values*	*Desirables*	*Score*	*Wt. Score*		*Score*	*Wt. Score*
Available in 3 months	10	Definitely	10	100	Probably	8	80
Long-term lease	6						
Nearby parking	9						
Close to restaurants	5						
Chicago "lakefront" character	3						
Reasonably low rent	4						
			Total			Total	

Adding up the weighted scores of both sites (see below) gives a snapshot of relative performance. It reveals that the two sites are close, very close. But the Michigan Avenue site is relatively better by a small margin, 287 to 277.

Alternatives			A. Michigan Ave.			B. Grand Ave.		
Desirables	Values	Desirables	Score	Wt. Score		Score	Wt. Score
Available in 3 months	10	Definitely	10	100	Possibly	8	80
Long-term lease	6	5 year	10	60	3 year	7	42
Nearby parking	9	Minimal	3	27	Plenty	10	90
Close to restaurants	5	The best	10	50	Almost none	2	10
Chicago "lakefront" character	3	Landmark	10	30	Brick warehouse	5	15
Reasonably low rent	4	Premium rent	5	20	Low rent	10	40
		Total	**287**		Total	**277**	

This snapshot is very helpful, but it's not the entire picture. There's still one more step before the decision can be made with assurance.

STEP FOUR

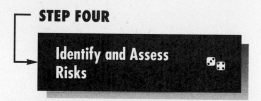

Identify and Assess Risks

Good decision makers take this extra step, called *Risk Analysis*. It can be a detailed probability analysis using sophisticated math. But more likely, what will work for you is some educated guessing more along the lines of "What do you think our competitors will do when we announce our price increase?"

Basically, there are two sources of risk information: One is criteria you may have overlooked that later appear to be critical; the other is new information that popped up as you explored the alternatives.

You need to look at both. You should take each alternative separately and try to predict what could go wrong.

Angela does this for her two remaining office sites.

At the Michigan Avenue site, parking is minimal. So employees could be late for work or spend time driving around looking for a parking space when they should be at their desks. Or, maybe even worse, customers could have a hard time finding a parking spot when they need to visit the office.

The other risk she sees as she looks over the Michigan Avenue data is that her company's going to be paying top dollar, in this case $250,000 a year. If times got tough and revenues for the firm fell, could that premium rent put the whole business in the red?

Risk Assessment

Alternative: **Michigan Avenue**

If... parking creates problems for employees,
Then... they may report late for work.

If... parking creates problems for customers,
Then... it may discourage customers from visiting the office.

If... the rent is close to the maximum limit,
Then... revenue fluctuations may put the business in the "red."

Then she looks at the Grand Avenue warehouse site.

Risk Assessment

Alternative: **Grand Avenue**

If... the office isn't completed on schedule,
Then... the bottom line contribution of Mr. Harris' office will be postponed.

If... restaurants are not easily accessible from the office,
Then... it may demoralize the employees.

The risks are that it wouldn't be finished on time, and that would not only upset Mr. Harris but would also be a disappointment to customers. At worst, it might mean this office wouldn't be making a contribution to the bottom line as soon as Mr. Harris wished. The other risk is that because of the lack of restaurants nearby, employee morale would sag. That could affect productivity.

Weigh the Risks

Hhhmmm! She now knows the risks. But how to weigh them? Every assessment of risk considers two factors: Probability and Seriousness.

Risk Assessment	Probability	Seriousness
Alternative: Michigan Avenue		
If... parking creates problems for employees, *Then...* they may report late for work.		
If... parking creates problems for customers, *Then...* it may discourage customers from visiting the office.		
If... the rent is close to the maximum limit, *Then...* revenue fluctuations may put the business in the "red."		
Alternative: Grand Avenue	Probability	Seriousness
If... the office isn't completed on schedule, *Then...* the bottom line contribution of Mr. Harris' office will be postponed.		
If... restaurants are not easily accessible from the office, *Then...* it may demoralize the employees.		

Probability is the leader's judgment about the *likelihood* that something will occur. Seriousness is its *impact* if it did happen. To keep it simple, Angela decides to score the risks high, medium, or low on Probability and Seriousness. She could put down a numerical score if she could quantify the risks.

Angela considers these risks and decides that Risk No. 1 at Michigan Avenue has a high Probability because parking problems there are unavoidable.

Risk Assessment	Probability	Seriousness
Alternative: __Michigan Avenue__		
If... parking creates problems for employees, *Then...* they may report late for work.	High	Medium
If... parking creates problems for customers, *Then...* it may discourage customers from visiting the office.	High	Low
If... the rent is close to the maximum limit, *Then...* revenue fluctuations may put the business in the "red."	Low	High

But she gives them only a medium Seriousness for employees and a low Seriousness for customers. That's because parking in New York, where they've been based, is even worse and the employees have learned to cope there without too much trouble. And in this business, salespeople usually drive to meet the customer; rarely does the customer visit the sales office. So the impact of the parking problem on the customer should be slight.

The Probability of the high rent causing serious financial problems for the company seems slight. A company rich enough to afford a Chicago expansion isn't likely to be torpedoed by $250,000, especially when the rent met the president's cost criteria. However, if it did happen that the rent became a financial Achilles' heel, that would be a major impact. So Angela ranks that as a low Probability but a high Seriousness. In other words, unlikely—but a big problem if it did occur.

On the other hand, if the Grand Avenue site isn't finished on time, that could cause real grief because Mr. Harris, the customers, and the employees are all counting on a firm start-up date. So Angela gives that a medium Probability and a high Seriousness.

Risk Assessment		
	Probability	Seriousness
Alternative: **Grand Avenue**		
If... the office isn't completed on schedule, *Then...* the bottom line contribution of Mr. Harris' office will be postponed.	Medium	High
If... restaurants are not easily accessible from the office, *Then...* it may demoralize the employees.	High	Low

The lack of a decent restaurant near Grand Avenue is a problem but not of the same magnitude. Employees could carpool to restaurants or bring their lunches, or the company might even be able to open a little snack bar, or something. At any rate, Angela thinks it unlikely that the employees, given all the other delights of working in Chicago, would be despondent over an imperfect lunch situation. So she ranks that a high Probability but low Seriousness.

So her risks stack up like this:

Risk Assessment		
	Probability	Seriousness
Alternative: **Michigan Avenue**		
If... parking creates problems for employees, *Then...* they may report late for work.	High	Medium
If... parking creates problems for customers, *Then...* it may discourage customers from visiting the office.	High	Low
If... the rent is close to the maximum limit, *Then...* revenue fluctuations may put the business in the "red."	Low	High
	Probability	Seriousness
Alternative: **Grand Avenue**		
If... the office isn't completed on schedule, *Then...* the bottom line contribution of Mr. Harris' office will be postponed.	Medium	High
If... restaurants are not easily accessible from the office, *Then...* it may demoralize the employees.	High	Low

So, Angela evaluates the two sites again. Neither is perfect. There's risk at both sites; that's life. But she's looking for manageable risk, acceptable risk. Once she's figured that out, she's ready to take the final Decision Making step.

Make the Decision

Angela concludes there's no risk that should override her tentative decision in favor of the Michigan Avenue site. The biggest risk (looking at both probability and seriousness) seems to be the chance that the Grand Avenue site can't be opened on time. The other risks at both sites either are unlikely or, if probable, will not have a high impact.

Angela sighs with satisfaction. It's taken some work and some discipline. But she's now confident she's come up with the right decision. There's nothing illogical about it. She can explain it clearly to anyone who asks. Most important, she has confidence that she's made the right decision for the right reasons.

She looks forward to her meeting with Mr. Harris where she'll tell him about the site she's picked and why. She knows he'll be impressed at her reasoning and her thoroughness.

She again rehearses in her mind the steps:

1. Know what you have to decide.

2. Establish and separate the criteria into Limits and Desirables.

3. Generate and compare alternatives.

4. Identify and Assess Risks.

Now that she is familiar with them, the steps have a logic and flow that's indisputable. She's sure that with the challenges ahead in running her own office in Chicago, she'll use Decision Making again and again.

Chapter **Four**

Skill 4 Plan Analysis
Assuring Success of a Decision

"Brian, you're only as good as your last miracle!" the boss said with a smile, thrusting a memo into your hand. "Or, to put it another way: What have you done for me lately? For sure, this'll test you."

He slapped you heartily, fondly on the back, and walked away. As he did, you scanned the memo and saw he wasn't joking. You'd just had one heck of a task dumped in your lap.

It's probably your fault, though. You're a victim of your own success. Maybe being a folk hero isn't all that it's cracked up to be. That's how you're still regarded by many after having pulled off what's known as "Brian's Marriott Miracle."

It was last summer and your billion-dollar software firm was hosting its annual "Western Regional Customer Appreciation Day" at a San Francisco-area Marriott hotel fronting a championship golf course. The biggest names in the Silicon Valley computer industry were invited to play in a golf tournament, followed by a fancy lunch. Expectations were high for a grand day—as well a chance to cement some solid business relationships.

Clear weather was predicted; you'd checked all the newscasts. But, as fate would have it, the skies suddenly opened up almost exactly at tee time and let loose with a deluge of almost Noah-like proportions. And it gave no sign of letting up.

Your boss, imagining 150 of the company's best customers forced to kill the whole morning playing video games in the hotel lounge, was beside himself. He was pulling out what little hair he has left when you said calmly, "Well, I do have a Plan B."

"What?"

"Sure, I always try to think ahead. I reserved one of the ball-rooms and had them clear out the furniture. I also brought some practice-putting cups; they're in the trunk of my car. Give me 15 minutes to mark off some distances on the banquet room carpeting with masking tape, and we'll have a putting competition set up in there. We can use the same prizes we were going to use for the tournament, plus we can even get a gourmet coffee cart rolled in there, if you'd like, with various brews to ward off the chill. How's that sound?"

You deduced by the vigorous nodding of your boss's head that you'd just come up with about the best idea since linoleum. The golfers seemed to think so, too. They stroked golf balls around the banquet room for hours and enthusiastically warded off the chill. Many of them said it was the most fun they'd had in months!

A few weeks later, not coincidentally, you were promoted to Director of Public Relations *and* Customer Service. Now with this new memo from your boss, you are going to be asked to earn your stripes again. This time, though, it will be more complicated.

MEMORANDUM

CONFIDENTIAL

From: Executive Vice President, Sales and Marketing
To: Director, Public Relations and Customer Service
Subject: South Korean Government Visit/Contract

Brian:

As you may know, we're expecting a Mr. Kim and his entourage for a very important visit. Mr. Kim has been named by President Li of South Korea to head a delegation coming to our facilities. San Corp., the Korean electronics giant, has approached us about providing word-processing software for the entire Korean government—all its agencies and auxiliaries.

San has helped the Korean government narrow its choices of suppliers from four to two. Informally, though, we understand we are San's first choice, and so this visit, if all goes well, should seal the deal. It, therefore, *must* go well.

It's potentially even a bigger contract than it may seem. North and South Korea, despite their publicly hostile stances, have cooperated on a few projects. There's reason to believe if we sell South Korea, we may get North Korea, too. That'd be worth another $50 million or so. (Several high-ranking North Korean officials will be on this tour, too, and San had made special arrangements with our State Department for processing them at the airport.)

Mr. Kim, and his party of 18, will arrive at San Francisco International on April 24 at 1:30 P.M. on Universal Flight #712.

I, along with our director of International Sales, will be escorting and entertaining Mr. Kim and his party and making the main presentation. But I want you to oversee the trip and tour logistics. I attached the rough agenda as we know it now.

We had hoped to have no publicity about this so that our competition wouldn't be alerted. But I just learned that the U.S. Secretary of Commerce is sending a representative, as is the Korea Trade Office of the State of California. Now that the cat's out of the bag, I went ahead and scheduled a press conference at the airport. Hope that works for you.

As I say, Brian, this is a big one. We can't afford any foul-ups of any kind. I'm counting on you to see that everything runs smoothly. After all, that's what you do so well!

Wow!

This is going to be a test, all right. The magnitude of the business deal, for one thing. Then there's the sort of hush-hush nature of the trip, with its ideological overtones. Multiple sites and a large number of people will complicate security. Besides, the involvement of Washington and Sacramento means possible political gamesmanship. Lots of chances for things to go wrong!

You won't be able to just quickly organize a putting competition. Brilliant though it may have been, that won't work this time!

But, you remind yourself as you take a calming breath, the same principles will apply. You did it once. You can do it again, albeit on a larger scale.

Figure out your objective. Come up with an intelligent plan and be ready to respond to challenges as they arise. That's Plan Analysis.

Nothing happens unless someone makes it happen. That's an axiom of leadership. But while making a decision removes uncertainty of one sort, it replaces it with others. The worry shifts from the present to the future.

The manager replaces the "What do I do now?" with other questions:

- "What's the plan?"
- "How do I make the plan work?"
- "What if it doesn't?"
- "How will I know if it isn't working?"

Too often, though, American firms reward those high-profile leaders who avoid asking those tough questions and instead pull some leadership sleight of hand to resolve a crisis. They are really not being praised as leaders, though, but as individuals who do a good job of damage control.

Truly effective leaders should avoid becoming better and better at damage control. Because no matter how good they get, they still have more impact if the damage is prevented in the first place.

Plan Analysis is the key to being proactive. Leaders who learn this skill will have less damage to deal with because they anticipate problems and side effects.

Just to prove this point, in our executive seminars I often ask, "What would you do if you were placed in charge of safety at a high-rise hotel in Manhattan and your first responsibility was to prevent the hotel from catching on fire and turning into a 'towering inferno'?"

Executives usually give me a list of ideas like these:

- Put in a sprinkler system.
- Install smoke alarms.
- Install heliport on roof for rescues.
- Forbid smoking in the hotel.
- Place fire extinguishers in every room.
- Install easily accessed fire escapes.

Then, as I repeat the question, I ask them to look again at their list, reminding them of the importance of prevention. These executives nod knowingly as they realize they've created a list of ideas to answer the wrong question.

I asked them "How would you prevent a fire?" not "How would you contain a fire" or "How would you limit damage from a fire?" The only preventive action on the list is the ban on smoking. The rest of the ideas aren't preventive actions, but contingent actions aimed at minimizing damage. Those will not prevent a fire at all, only contain it or help evacuate the building.

Obvious Signs

The odd thing about most corporate or career setbacks is that signs of the growing problem are usually obvious. But managers are still caught unaware and fail to either prevent the disaster or have a contingency plan ready.

A major oil company, for example, faced the gargantuan task of moving an offshore drilling rig from the Indian Ocean to the North Sea. The firm devised a complex plan to deploy a fleet of tugs to move the huge rig around the Cape of Good Hope and up the coasts of Africa and western Europe to the North Sea.

There were many adventures and quite a few mishaps along the way. In fact, it was a rare day that something didn't go awry, often resulting in panic and other irrational responses. The firm's training division decided to use this real-life project as a learning exercise for developing new managers.

As part of the training, these relatively inexperienced leaders were given the basic plan for moving the oil rig and then asked to list all the potential problems they thought were worth worrying about. The result? Over 50 percent of the problems that actually occurred were identified by these novices. In other words, at least half the problems were readily foreseeable.

That caught senior management's eye! Why hadn't experienced hands at the firm done a better job of anticipating? A careful Plan Analysis, the top officials concluded, could have saved the firm more than $300,000.

When you master Plan Analysis, you learn how to make and monitor plans in a way that will head off a crisis before it occurs. You learn how to state the plan, find the critical areas, identify ways to *prevent problems*, develop backup plans in case something goes wrong, and then build in alarms to trigger those backup plans.

But Plan Analysis is more than just problem prevention. It also allows you to anticipate potential *opportunities*. A task force at a major Canadian telecommunications company, for instance, devised a new performance-appraisal program. While eager to put it into effect, the group decided first to use Plan Analysis.

What it found was that the launch date would conflict with the year-end budget wrap-up, that the plan omitted branch plants that already were feeling ignored by headquarters, and that translating the plan into French, as required by Canadian law, was going to take a lot longer than originally believed.

In addition to these problems, an opportunity also was discovered: The personnel department was about to issue a new supervisor's manual. It made a lot of sense to launch the two projects jointly.

New information sessions were added to include the branch offices, and by delaying the start-up long enough to merge the performance-appraisal project with the new supervisor's manual, the firm gained enough time to do the French translations and avoid the conflict with the budget wrap-up.

So, by taking the time to ask the right Plan Analysis questions, the task force avoided foreseeable problems, seized on opportunities, and made for a stronger launch of both programs.

The Four Basic Steps

There's an old saying among sailors that the superior skipper is the one who uses his superior knowledge so that his superior skills won't be necessary. To put it another way, if he's really on top of a situation, he'll avoid getting into a jam.

Similarly, good leaders have well-honed sensing systems to allow them to detect concerns long before they become crises.

So Plan Analysis is a technique—and a way of thinking—that lets you intelligently prepare for both problems and opportunities. It helps you get things done more quickly, with less stress and fewer headaches.

In simplest form the steps of Plan Analysis are as follows:

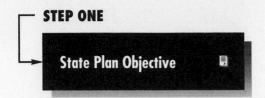

STEP ONE

State Plan Objective

Before you can do anything in life—cook an omelet, run a giant corporation, change the government—you've got to know what you're trying to accomplish.

So, when making a plan, you should first state the objective in one or two sentences, making certain to include the desired result. This gives you a clear picture of what you are trying to achieve and helps keep you on track during the planning process.

No matter how simple or how complex, all plans are alike in this one respect: They show what must be done to achieve a certain objective.

And the first question is this: What's the objective?

Again, you're Brian, the PR guy at the big software firm. The Koreans' visit has been dumped in your lap. What will your plan try to accomplish? What's the objective?

Plan Objective

To ensure a successful visit of Korean officials on April 24–28. The trip should give exposure to our firm and community without embarrassing or inconveniencing our guests.

That's simple enough, even if the plan itself probably won't be. However, Brian's experience in public relations should be a great help in preparing his plan.

For starters, he looks at the agenda his boss has already handed him:

SCHEDULED VISIT OF MR. KIM (Page 1)

Wednesday, April 24

1:30 P.M.   Arrival at SFO, Universal Flight #712.

Press conference at VIP Lounge. Motorcade to hotel for check-in.

4:30 P.M.   Reception with San Francisco mayor at The Top of the Mark.

5:45 P.M.   Travel by motorcade to private bayside club in Marin County.

8:30 P.M.   Evening cruise on San Francisco Bay, leaving from Tiburon pier.

11:15 P.M.   Return by limo to hotel.

Thursday, April 25

7:30–
11:30 A.M.   Golf at Twin Oaks Country Club.

1:00 P.M.   Tour of our corporate facilities (Manufacturing, Customer Support, Usability Lab, Selected Facilities, Hard Disk).

Will include buffet luncheon in executive suite and slide show in board room.

6:00 P.M.   Dinner and floor show on Nob Hill.

Friday, April 26

Morning free.

1:00 P.M.   Poolside lunch at hotel. Afternoon tour bus to Napa Valley wineries.

Saturday, April 27

8:00 A.M.   Limousine pickup at hotel.

9:00 A.M.   Conference in executive suite.

Each Executive Vice President will make a 30-minute presentation, followed by 15-minute Q & A.

1:00 P.M.   Catered lunch in executive suite.

SCHEDULED VISIT OF MR. KIM (Page 2)

2:30 P.M.   Department and function meetings with Korean technical advisor and heads of our departments:

CIS, Account Management Teams, Software
Development, International Documentation,
International R & D.

Evening free.

Tuesday, April 28

8:00 A.M.   Farewell breakfast at hotel. Valedictory remarks by CEO.

10:45 A.M.   Airport limousine pickup.

12:45 P.M.   Universal flight #718 departs SFO for Seoul.

Okay, you now know the objective, and you've got the raw material for an initial action plan.

How complicated is a plan? Well, it can be anything from a mental checklist to a critical path diagram. Devising it is where your experience begins to show. Here you use your savvy to pinpoint ways to achieve your desired results. The best planning is proactive: It anticipates what could go wrong before the problems arise.

STEP TWO

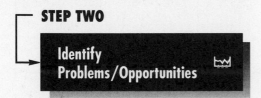

Identify
Problems/Opportunities

Looking at the tentative but ambitious schedule, Brian right away sees many potential problems. For starters, that airport press conference upon arrival is a perfect setup for protesters, for special-interest groups, or maybe even for the competition to show up and do something to embarrass the firm or its Korean guests. Besides, having the North Koreans there is sure to be a political lightning rod.

Similarly, Brian wonders if there might be embarrassing questions from reporters that night when boarding the boat at the public dock in Tiburon. It wouldn't be good for the company to be connected, however peripherally, with a brutal Communist regime.

Something else Brian notices: Many of these events are fairly closely scheduled and often near rush hour. Given Bay Area traffic, he may need to take steps to ensure that the Korean visitors don't end up stuck on Highway 101.

One other potential nightmare occurs to Brian: With such a large entourage of non-English speakers visiting so many sites, think how bad it would be if one or more of them got lost. It could happen if Brian's not careful.

There is a lot to be done! But better to grapple with those prospects now than when the Koreans arrive or, worse yet, after the problems occur.

Many opportunities are missed because we aren't ready to take advantage of them. You may have heard an anguished executive say, "If *only* I'd known!" That's the refrain of a manager who lacks foresight. That isn't so likely with Plan Analysis.

Should problems and opportunities be simultaneously listed? Actually, better results occur if you tally problems and opportunities separately. It seems to help clarify thinking and produce more complete lists. Another helpful hint for compiling either problems or opportunities is to talk to others who might see threats or openings that you're blind to.

Looking now at the Koreans' schedule, Brian immediately sees several opportunities; for one, the private reception with the Mayor of San Francisco at The Top of the Mark. If handled right, that could bring some good PR.

Similarly, because these high-profile Koreans are going to be here for most of four days, maybe Brian can help bridge the cultural gap. Perhaps he can help them feel more comfortable and also put his firm in a good light as being interested in and connected with the Korean-American community. Brian remembers meeting a highly ranked professional golfer in San Mateo who is a Korean-American. Perhaps he could be invited to the Thursday golf tournament. If he's not available, maybe another prominent Korean-American would be.

So now Brian has got what seems to be good lists of key Potential Problems and Opportunities.

Problems/ Opportunities	Prevention/ Facilitation	Backup	Alarms
Protests and/or embarrassing questions at airport			
Protests and/or embarrassing questions at Tiburon pier			
Freeway gridlock during motorcades			
Lost visitors			
Mayor's reception (opportunity)			
Build cultural bridges to Korean-Americans (opportunity)			

Now that he's listed his Potential Problems and Potential Opportunities, Brian's next task is to figure out how he's going to deal with them.

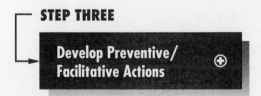

STEP THREE

Develop Preventive/ Facilitative Actions ⊕

It's not enough to know what problems and opportunities lurk ahead. Taking control and being proactive means trying to avert the problems and seizing the opportunities.

So looking at the list of potential problems, Brian tries to come up with preventive actions. As for the potential opportunities, he tries to come up with facilitative actions.

Problems/ Opportunities	Prevention/ Facilitation	Backup	Alarms
Protests and/or embarrassing questions at airport	Meet with protest groups. Brief Mr. Kim and prepare responses to sensitive queries. Alert airport security. Locate emergency exits.		
Protests and/or embarrassing questions at Tiburon pier	Meet with protest groups. Brief Mr. Kim and prepare responses to sensitive queries. Alert Tiburon police.		
Freeway gridlock during motorcades	Educate drivers about alternate routes. Put walkie-talkies in cars.		
Lost visitors	Put local guide in each car. Produce, distribute list of visitors. Require frequent headcounts.		
Mayor's reception (opportunity)	Alert "friendly" media.		
Build cultural bridges to Korean-Americans (opportunity)	Invite Korean-American golf pro to Thursday outing.		

STEP FOUR

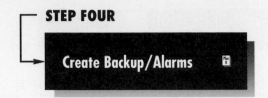

Create Backup/Alarms

Murphy's Law is always on the books. It will never be repealed. Even the most careful planning can't guarantee flawless implementation. So you also need a backup, or contingent, action and a way to know when it's called for.

If something goes wrong, you'd like to be able to move into a previously developed backup position. If the problem you're protecting against is sufficient to be worth managing, you ought to develop a contingent action that answers the question, if this problem arises, what will I do?

Ideally, you'll never have to use it, just as you hope you never have to make a claim on your fire insurance or find out if your automobile air bag works. By definition, it's a second-best action, a safety release that should be avoided unless absolutely required, like a skydiver's reserve chute.

Likewise, there's an equal need to be ready to exploit your opportunities. Any time you increase your advertising, for example, you better make sure that your salespeople are prepared to follow up new leads.

In any event, failure to plan for contingencies means you could miss an opportunity, or a problem could worsen greatly before being dealt with.

So, if you were Brian, you'd list your contingent actions like this:

Problems/ Opportunities	Prevention/ Facilitation	Backup	Alarms
Protests and/or embarrassing questions at airport	Meet with protest groups. Brief Mr. Kim and prepare responses to sensitive queries. Alert airport security. Locate emergency exits.	Airport security to disband protesters. Cancel press conference.	
Protests and/or embarrassing questions at Tiburon pier	Meet with protest groups. Brief Mr. Kim and prepare responses to sensitive queries. Alert Tiburon police.	Tiburon Police disband protestors—allow easy access to boat.	
Freeway gridlock during motorcades	Educate drivers about alternate routes. Put walkie-talkies in cars.	Take alternative routes.	
Lost visitors	Put local guide in each car. Produce, distribute list of visitors. Require frequent headcounts.	Alert police's Korean liaison. Distribute description of lost visitor to media and police.	
Mayor's reception (opportunity)	Alert "friendly" media.	Send news release to local/national media.	
Build cultural bridges to Korean-Americans (opportunity)	Invite Korean-American golf pro to Thursday outing.	Plan trip to Korea to visit them.	

So Brian now knows what he's going to do if things go bad or even how to get a leg up if things go exceptionally well. What he still needs is a contingency alarm that will tell him when to activate these backup systems.

Every contingency must have an alarm. It's a predetermined signal that tells you to shift into the contingency. Without it, there's no guarantee about the potential impact or timing of the contingency.

An alarm isn't just a milepost or a point in time. It's the occurrence or non-occurrence of certain events at a prescribed time. Good leaders are consistently monitoring plans. The failure of raw material to arrive by a specified date, for example, may trigger reallocation of workers to a different production line. A baseball manager might automatically bring in the relief pitcher if there's two men on base and less than two outs any time after the seventh inning.

This works for opportunities as well as problems. Any opportunity missed can be as serious as a problem we try to prevent.

Let's look at alarms that might be used in the case of the Koreans' visit.

Problems/ Opportunities	Prevention/ Facilitation	Backup	Alarms
Protests and/or embarrassing questions at airport	Meet with protest groups. Brief Mr. Kim and prepare responses to sensitive queries. Alert airport security. Locate emergency exits.	Airport security to disband protesters. Cancel press conference.	Demonstrators appear early. Gauge media queries to be overly hostile.
Protests and/or embarrassing questions at Tiburon pier	Meet with protest groups. Brief Mr. Kim and prepare responses to sensitive queries. Alert Tiburon police.	Tiburon Police disband protestors—allow easy access to boat.	Police report unusual activity in vicinity of pier. Reporters appear.
Freeway gridlock during motorcades	Educate drivers about alternate routes. Put walkie-talkies in cars.	Take alternative routes.	Highway Patrol reports major problems.
Lost visitors	Put local guide in each car. Produce, distribute list of visitors. Require frequent headcounts.	Alert police's Korean liaison. Distribute description of lost visitor to media and police.	Someone not present during headcount.
Mayor's reception (opportunity)	Alert "friendly" media.	Send news release to local/national media.	Reception goes exceptionally well.
Build cultural bridges to Korean-Americans (opportunity)	Invite Korean-American golf pro to Thursday outing.	Plan trip to Korea to visit them.	Much headway is made during visit.

There! Brian's got his backup plan in place. He knows what he's going to do if things go wrong—and precisely what it will take to trigger those contingencies.

That doesn't mean the Koreans' visit will go perfectly. Nothing that complicated does. But it does mean that by analyzing the project in advance, Brian feels ready to respond to challenges as they arise. He's taken all reasonable precautions to prevent disaster and maximize opportunities.

Plan Analysis requires an investment of time, thought, and effort. But it's an investment that brings big returns. A key to proactivity, this skill gives a payoff not only operationally, but also in peace of mind.

At its best, Plan Analysis functions like radar that signals incoming problems in time for you to minimize their impact, using basic tools for prevention and backup. Again, the simple questions to ask are as follows:

- "What's the plan?"
- "How do I make the plan work?"
- "What if it doesn't?"
- "How will I know if it isn't working?"

Answering these questions in advance takes a little time. But over the long run, it makes for not only a smoother operation, but less stress and fewer headaches for everyone. Do this consistently and you will be the leader: I promise you, everyone will want you on their team.

Brian squints into the distance, seeing acres of grass and trees— and somewhere out there is his golf ball. He hooked badly off the seventh tee. But it doesn't matter because, overall, things are going wonderfully.

The Koreans arrived yesterday as scheduled, breezed through the press conference, and were a hit at the mayor's reception. The bay cruise went off without a hitch (except for one San official who got a bit seasick). So far, there have been no traffic problems of consequence and none of the Koreans have gotten lost. In fact, everyone—including Brian—is enjoying golf on a beautiful spring day.

The Korean-American golf pro from San Mateo jumped at the chance to be a goodwill ambassador. He's been joking with the visitors and giving golf pointers in Korean. Both Brian's boss and Mr. Kim are delighted that Brian came up with that idea.

Brian is enjoying the golfing break. He considers it a triumph of Plan Analysis that he is able to be there at all. But even more than the recreation, he enjoyed the boss's look of pleasant surprise when Brian showed up with his clubs.

"Nice to see you, Brian," the boss said with a smile. "It's been a dandy visit so far. Everything under control on your end?"

"All the bases are covered," Brian said confidently, sensing another feather being placed in his cap.

Chapter **Five**

Skill 5 Innovation
Creating Something Better

Here's the stark reality of today's world: If you're not moving forward, you're losing ground. That's true of individuals and companies alike. In other words, just being good enough, isn't.

Leaders who are out in front know that. As a result, they keep raising their standards. Even if some of their choices don't work out, they still charge ahead, always thinking, adapting, innovating.

Or, as Peter F. Drucker wrote in *The Harvard Business Review,* "Core competencies are different for every organization . . . But every organization—not just businesses—needs one core competence: innovation."

Innovation is Skill No. 5. It helps you figure out what to do when you need to do something you're not doing now. This involves exercising, you might say, a whole different set of mental muscles. In earlier chapters, the skills were about sorting through masses of facts and then evaluating the data. Innovation, though, is about making a decision when there doesn't seem to be any traditional alternatives, when you've got to create the options, as it were, from the ground up.

But it's not just idle daydreaming we're talking about. Creativity must occur within some framework to be useful. Totally, goalless think tanks are a luxury few can afford. Instead, the key to Innovation is to combine rational process with the creative process. The best creativity springs from both the left and right sides of the brain; it's focused on a specific problem, yet is free-floating in its associations. The form the solution takes may be totally unspecified—but the goal must be sharply defined.

And that's the challenge.

You're the marketing manager for Mistachio Winery in Upstate New York. For five years, you've been selling your 6-ounce, individual bottles of red, white, and rosé wine to TransAmerican Airways. This product is one of your most successful.

The dollar volume from TransAmerican is considerable. Equally important, the arrangement keeps your profile high among the upscale traveling public. Finally, the long-term nature of the contract permits substantial production runs, ensuring a good profit margin on these small bottles.

But there's a problem. TransAmerican has come to you with a concern about the tall, thin bottles. The shape creates loading problems for the airline, uses too much valuable storage space, and causes the bottles to be unstable on the passengers' trays.

What are you going to do? You don't have the foggiest! This has never come up before. Haven't wine bottles *always* been this shape? In any event, you absolutely need to keep this account. You'll have to think of something.

The Creativity "Sandwich"

The essence of Innovation is what I call, for short, a creativity "sandwich."

Let me explain. One of the most enduring fallacies of life is that people and groups are either creative or rational: daydreamers, brainstormers, "imagineerers" on one hand or pragmatic, hard-nosed, results-oriented practitioners on the other.

That's highly simplistic. In truth, very little pure research into totally new directions ever amounts to much. Breakthroughs rarely are spontaneous discoveries accompanied by shouts of "Eureka!"

Instead, productive creativity almost always is focused on improving existing products and practices. One major R&D lab in the telecommunications industry, for example, spends 90 percent of its research funds on what it calls "mission-oriented research." Only 10 percent is spent on nondirected research. As a result, this lab is recognized worldwide as a leader in its field.

The first step in Innovation is to identify opportunities and set goals and criteria. These are analytical tasks. But next, based on those goals and criteria, comes the creativity: brainstorming the new ideas. Then you sandwich those with further analysis to sort out potential solutions and pinpoint which ideas can be made into a reality—analysis/creativity/analysis.

Thus, the creativity "sandwich."

A small, but important point: All this talk about creativity, about Innovation, is moot unless the firm or organization fosters a climate that allows mistakes, illogic, diversions, unsupported ideas, and other group behavior that is outside the norm. That doesn't mean the organization has to be undisciplined; on the contrary, the more rational an organization, the greater chance it has of moving creativity to Innovation. Innovation is successfully applied creativity.

Without ground rules encouraging a great degree of freedom, Innovation will not flourish. If the culture is "But we've always done it this way" or "That's not our style" or "We can't do anything too radical," then Innovation cannot be effective. If your people are afraid of going "too far," they're unlikely to go far enough. The importance of climate setting cannot be exaggerated.

There's a related problem at companies with a cold climate for Innovation, and it's what I term the "it won't work" syndrome. This is a favorite device used by those dedicated to organizational obstacles: They always find a flaw somewhere in any proposal. Thus, they undermine the credibility of the entire solution for the sake of a minor point. This gives them an apparent feeling of accomplishment but often at the expense of progress.

In truth, though, most workable solutions result from taking the best from several competing ideas. So it's unrealistic to expect any one alternative to be perfect at first glance. Again, when searching for possible solutions, you need to have an open, nonjudgmental attitude and not eliminate choices that aren't ideal. As you've doubtlessly found out by now, life is not a succession of optimal solutions!

Speaking of life not being optimal, TransAmerican officials met with you and outlined their concerns about your wine bottles:

- Because many passengers request wine, the airline must keep a large inventory of Mistachio bottles on each plane. But the tall, thin shape of the bottles creates loading problems—a number of cases have been damaged—and too much precious storage space is used up.

- The bottles are top-heavy and when there's air turbulence, they sometimes tip over or fall out of the preformed depressions in the passenger tray tables. Passengers have complained.

TransAmerica stopped short of threatening to switch suppliers. But they did ask you to develop an alternative. The airline makes a good profit on wine sales and TransAmerica's managers want a solution that's acceptable to its passengers.

The Steps of Innovation

Given the need for Innovation and the right climate, there are four basic steps to follow, or four standard questions to be answered.

- **Objective:** What is the end result desired?
- **Criteria:** What are your limitations?
- **Ideas:** What new ideas can we generate?
- **Solutions:** How can we combine or leverage ideas to get to workable solutions?

1 State Innovation Objective

2 Develop Design Criteria

3 Generate Ideas

4 Create Potential Solutions

STEP ONE

State Innovation Objective

First, you need to clarify the Innovation opportunity by deciding its aim.

The following are several points to keep in mind when crafting this statement:

- Usually this is a statement beginning with a key phrase, such as "How best to..."

- State the goal in *positive* terms. Stating it negatively (such as "Reduce costs on...") will narrowly restrict thinking and will limit your ability to come up with innovative ideas.

- Be as open-ended as possible while still providing focus. For example, "How best to design a transportation vehicle for the next century" is better than "How best to design an automobile for the next century."

Then look at your objective. Is it too restrictive? Too broad? Can it be stated more simply? More positively? Does it specify an end result, or does it box you in by dictating a method for achieving the goal?

For example, let's return to the problem of the airline wine bottles. TransAmerican has said it has trouble with the tall, thin shape of the small wine bottles. So what is your objective?

Well, you could state your goal this way: "How best to improve storage capacity and stability of wine bottles." But that presumes bottles are the only way to go. Bottles are what you use now and, indeed, have always used. But perhaps that's too limiting. Maybe there's another sort of container you haven't thought about that would be more easily shipped and stored and more stable in flight.

So a better statement of objective would be: "How best to respond to TransAmerican's concern about wine bottles." That gives you a wider universe of possibilities without becoming vague or fuzzy. Once you have settled on your objective, you're ready for the second step in Innovation.

STEP TWO

Develop Design Criteria ✓

Before you can generate ideas and solutions, you must know what specific results are desired and any restrictions that must be met. Such guidelines provide direction and focus.

The criteria will make idea generation easier. They will also be a gauge of how feasible the solutions are and whether they actually will work. At this stage it's helpful to gather opinions from numerous people. You will want your criteria to reflect the needs of the organization and the people who will need to approve and support an innovation. But you will also want to hear from those who will use it.

The following are some hints for developing your criteria:

- Begin with the statement, "Whatever we do should…"

- State the criteria positively. (For example, use the criterion "Whatever we do should maintain or enhance our market image," rather than "Whatever we do should not interfere with our present market image.")

- Describe the objective, not the method for achieving it. (For example, "Whatever we do should maximize worker participation," not "…should involve Quality Circles.")

- Limit each criterion to one objective only. Avoid compound criteria. ("Whatever we do should increase productivity and make workers feel important" is a compound criterion.) Keeping them simple spurs more ideas and ensures the widest range of solutions.

- Keep the number manageable. A good rule of thumb is to list no more than 8 or 10 criteria. Too many can paralyze the process with restrictions and constraints.

In the case of the wine bottles, what are the criteria?

Well, your client, TransAmerican, made clear what they want. They want bottles that are easier to store and ship and that won't fall over during flight. They also said the new container had to be acceptable to the passengers.

So, for starters, you have those criteria. But you can also think of more of your own. For example, you want to maintain your high market exposure. You want to keep the production costs low. And, now that you think about it, it would be great if you came up with a way to market this same small container of wine to clients other than the airlines.

So you draw up a list like this:

Wine Bottle	
	Whatever we do should...
	1. Be more space-effective
	2. Be more stable on passenger tray tables
	3. Be easier to ship and handle
	4. Optimize market exposure
	5. Not cost any more to produce
	6. Be marketable to other clients
	7. Be acceptable to TransAmerican passengers

Not all criteria are of equal worth. That's because some are better springboards for ideas than others. So for the best Innovation, you should select just those criteria that seem likely to stimulate a lot of thought.

Criteria that do that are usually more open-ended. They also relate directly to the Objective Statement, and they avoid constraints (such as budget or time restrictions).

The criteria that don't meet those tests often can serve better as feasibility tests later in the process. So let's go through the list again, checking off those that seem to be key.

Wine Bottle

Whatever we do should...

✓ 1.	Be more space-effective
✓ 2.	Be more stable on passenger tray tables
✓ 3.	Be easier to ship and handle
4.	Optimize market exposure
5.	Not cost any more to produce
6.	Be marketable to other clients
✓ 7.	Be acceptable to TransAmerican passengers

We selected the first three and number seven as key criteria because they relate directly to the Objective, are open-ended and stimulating, and avoid constraints.

"Optimize market exposure" and "Be marketable to other clients" were not selected as key criteria because they don't relate to the objective—that is, they don't reflect TransAmerican's concerns. And "Not cost any more to produce" was not included because of its limiting nature.

Now you've completed the first phase of the analysis. The next step is the meat of the "sandwich": the creativity.

STEP THREE

Generate Ideas   !

This is where you can use your natural creativity. It's not easy; it requires a shift of perception. You must suspend judgment about how things *ought* to be. Instead, you should focus on what they *could* be. This means taking greater risks in your thinking.

This is another stage at which you often will want to talk with others. Group sessions are very helpful because they generate a lot of ideas quickly. To begin, a group should review the key criteria and say, "Maybe we could…"

A good technique to use here is brainstorming. That's where a group spontaneously tosses out ideas, regardless of how preliminary or far-fetched they may seem. In fact, for nearly 80 percent of your Innovation challenges, you should be able to use brainstorming.

The following are some principles of brainstorming:

- **Defer judgment.** If people feel they must evaluate their own ideas before they suggest them, you won't get many. Similarly, if people judge the ideas of others, the idea flow will be impeded. But you can defer judgment by suggesting ideas without concern for their value, feasibility, or significance.

- **Be as wild as possible.** A wild or crazy idea rarely ends up as part of the innovative solution. But it can help you and a group take off in an entirely new direction. Wild ideas can propel you out of a rut and help you avoid the most obvious solutions. This is often the most difficult principle to follow because it requires everybody to defer judgment at all costs.

- **Generate as many ideas as possible.** Pushing for quantity can help generate good, high-quality ideas. The more ideas you come up with, the more likely you'll discover a diamond in the rough.

- **Build and improve ideas.** As you and the group listen to the ideas of others, you'll find it gets easier to come up with further new ideas or to improve on those already suggested. This helps avoid idea stagnation, which can occur if you try to think of only brand-new ideas.

Other Brainstorming Techniques

What follows are some other techniques to help you brainstorm better.

Idea Quota

To stretch your minds, set a goal that states your group's idea quantity—a quantity that is *more* than what you can easily generate. That will get you focusing on quantity, and that in turn will force you to think more broadly.

Channeling

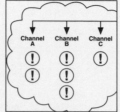

To encourage listening, you and other group members listen to the "channels" —the main themes—inherent in ideas rather than the ideas themselves. Then let the channels trigger new ideas in different areas. For example, brainstorming about parking might trigger the idea of bonuses for those using public transit. The bonus idea then becomes the trigger for bonuses for carpools, which could trigger bonuses for people who buy their own computers and work from home, and so on.

Chain Letter

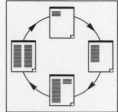

A letter goes to each group member—one by one. Each member writes down his or her ideas and passes the letter along to the next member. This often is appropriate when the group is not available to meet, when the potential for conflict is high, and/or when group members want ideas to be anonymous. Rerouting the letter encourages further idea building.

Graffiti Chart

A chart is posted in a central location and group members are encouraged to write down ideas about a topic as they pass by. This is a way to gather input quickly from a large number of people.

Nominal Group Technique

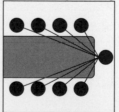

Each group member is called upon in a separate order to express an idea. This helps promote robust, balanced contribution from the group. More passive members are encouraged to participate "in turn," while traditionally outspoken members are discouraged from dominating the session.

Notestorming

Each member of a group writes ideas on a stick-on note. Each note is posted on a chart for group evaluation. This yields many ideas quickly, preserves anonymity, and may forestall premature arguments.

Okay, you've got your folks brainstorming about the Mistachio wine problem. You're casting the net broadly, striving for a lot of ideas. You're trying for some wild ideas, too, as well as piggybacking on existing ideas.

What did you come up with? Well, you defined two main groupings of key criteria: "Be more space effective" and "Be more stable on passenger trays."

Then you came up with a list of innovative ideas for each. Wow! You're pretty pleased with them. They're certainly creative.

For the space effectiveness criterion, the ideas look like this:

Wine Bottle

●	**"Be more space effective"**
	Serve dehydrated wine in foil packages.
	Package wine in large boxes and serve by the glass.
	Pour individual glasses from large bottles on attendants' trays.
	Have passengers drink before boarding plane.
	Devise "wine strips"—tear off and chew, release the wine.
	Store wine in huge collapsable jugs in wings of plane.
●	Store bottles end-to-end rather than upright.
	Ask passengers to buy a bottle at the gate before boarding.
	Serve wine in tablet form.
	Serve wine in cups sealed with foil.
	Store wine in large, square jugs mounted on attendants' tray.
	Use present bottles, but pack them in stackable foam boxes.

For the stability criterion, the ideas look like this:

Wine Bottle

"Be more stable on passenger trays"
Devise a pyramid-shaped bottle.
Attach bottle to tray with adhesive strips.
Weight bottom of bottle.
Ask airline to redesign the tray.
Use cup instead of a bottle.
Install bottle holder on seat rest.
Serve wine in individual bota bag.
Install a wine vending machine in back of seat.
Serve wine in plastic bag with a straw.
Put microscope suction cups on bottom of bottle.
Serve "winesicles."
Hang plastic wine bags from ceiling w/long straws for passengers.
Serve in short, squat individual-sized bottles.

Hhhmmm! Long lists. Definitely some unusual ideas there. Wild ideas, too, such as serving wine in tablet form or as "winesicles." Then there are ideas—for example, pyramid-shaped bottles—followed by an idea that builds upon that, such as "Weight bottom of the bottle." And there are instances of channeling, for instance, alternatives to the traditional bottle and ways to make the present bottle stay on the tray.

STEP FOUR

Create Potential Solutions

Only rarely does a single bright idea result in significant Innovation. Instead, most Innovation comes from creatively combining a number of good, workable ideas and then refining them into a solution:

How do you do that? Well, first, you go over your list of ideas and pick out the best, most interesting, or most novel. You toss out those wild ideas used only for stimulating thought.

Don't be too harsh on ideas at this point. Remember, you still want a variety of ideas. You just want to narrow the list. If you're too selective at this point, you'll limit creativity.

But once you've shortened the list, start grouping the remaining ideas according to theme. Usually, you can find three or four broad themes that are clear and obvious. Under each, list all the potential ideas that relate to that theme.

Hints: You may have a theme called "Others" that contains miscellaneous ideas not naturally falling into another group. And it's okay to have ideas repeated under different themes.

Once you've got your ideas grouped under themes, you can begin to combine them into potential solutions. Looking at our ideas for the wine-bottle problem, we can see four main themes.

A. Bottle Design

B. No Storage on Plane

C. Improved Storage

D. Nonbottle Packaging

So we group the best ideas under those themes. That list looks like this:

A. *Bottle Design*
- Pyramid shape.

- Weighted bottom.
- Large, square jugs on attendants' trays.
- Short, squat individual-sized bottles.

B. *No Storage on Plane*
- Have passengers drink before boarding plane.
- Ask passengers who wish to drink to buy bottle at gate before boarding.

C. *Improved Storage*
- Store bottles end-to-end instead of upright.
- Pack in foam boxes.
- Pack wine in large boxes and serve by the glass.

D. *Nonbottle Packaging*
- Cups sealed with foil.
- Individual bota bags.
- Package in large boxes and serve by the glass.
- Serve in plastic bag with straw.

So what have we done here? We've eliminated those ideas that would be highly unacceptable: dehydrated wine, wine strips, winesicles, wine in tablet form, and wine jugs swinging from the ceiling of the airplane.

And we've eliminated those that involve unavailable resources, are beyond our control, or would take too much time: developing wine vending machines for the back of the seats, getting the airline to redesign the trays, or storing huge collapsible wine jugs in the wings of the plane.

But we've tried not to eliminate ideas simply because they've never been tried before. The key, of course, is to select those ideas with the most potential without excluding viable ones. Ideas such as "Have passengers drink before boarding plane" and "Serve wine in individualized bota bags" were retained.

A key to Innovation, as we've seen, is withholding judgment. This is essential for developing the greatest number of creative ideas. But you can't withhold judgment forever. Once you've developed a number of potential solutions, you've got to begin evaluating them. Doing so also gives you a chance to improve and refine those possible solutions—and even come up with some additional ones.

You may choose to combine existing solutions into one better solution. So, in this sense, evaluation frequently entails still more creativity.

What determines whether a potential solution is likely to work? Well, for starters, it must be feasible. Second, it's got to perform in the desired way. And, third, it can't involve unacceptable risk.

Assessing Feasibility

To assess feasibility, you measure the solution against the criteria you developed earlier. As was true in Decision Making, you will want to separate the criteria into Limits, absolutely essential requirements, and Desirables, those standards that would be nice to meet but are not required.

Measure the solution against each of the Limits. Does it satisfy each Limit? If not, you must decide either to modify the solution to satisfy the Limits or eliminate that solution as unworkable.

Evaluating Performance

Next, you evaluate the likely performance of the remaining solutions. You do this by measuring the solution against the Desirables and then discussing the strengths and weaknesses of the solution in each area.

Refinements may be needed to improve the performance of the solutions.

Calculating Risk

Here you identify what could go wrong with a solution, figuring out the likelihood and impact of each potential risk. Again, this may lead to your making refinements to some, or all, of the solutions.

Naturally, most innovations entail risk. So you can't fret about each and every one. Instead, you need to sort out major risks in terms of probability and seriousness.

Ask yourself what risk, if any, would almost surely happen. If it did happen, would the impact be serious? If you find a probable risk with a serious impact, you'll need to refine the solution in a way to remove, or reduce, the risk.

Once you've evaluated the feasibility, performance, and risk, you can make your final refinements. This can be one of the most creative steps of the process.

You'll probably want to try to build one idea, or a combination of ideas, into the ultimate solution. Using group brainstorming again may help to hone the solutions.

Finding the best solution often means searching for a way to add or delete something from the solution. And often it's something rather obvious. For example, one project team recommended a new design for a product to bring in more profits. However, one of the Limits criteria was that production time could increase by no more than 5 percent, and the new design increased production time by 10 percent. Rather than just scrapping the design, they successfully sought to modify the production process. After just a slight change there, the team found it could limit the production time increase to 3 percent while still maintaining the cost savings of the new design.

Back to Mistachio. What are the semifinal, refined solutions? We return to our potential solutions listed by themes:

A. *Bottle Design*
- Pyramid shape.
- Weighted bottom.
- Large, square jugs on attendants' trays .
- Short, squat individual-sized bottles.

B. *No Storage on Plane*
- Have passengers drink before boarding plane.
- Ask passengers who wish to drink to buy bottle at gate before boarding.

C. *Improved Storage*
- Store bottles end-to-end instead of upright.
- Pack in foam boxes.
- Pack wine in large boxes and serve by the glass.

D. *Nonbottle Packaging*
- Cups sealed with foil.
- Individual bota bags.
- Package in large boxes and serve by the glass.
- Serve in plastic bag with straw.

We come up with four semifinal solutions. Each is a combination of ideas from one of the four themes.

1. Provide wine in shorter, squat individual-sized bottles, stored end-to-end in foam boxes.
2. Provide wine in full-sized boxes; attendant pours individual glasses.
3. Provide wine in individual cardboard containers with vacuum-packed foil interiors.
4. Provide wine in plastic cups sealed with foil.

Completing the Process

Then we complete the process by identifying the Limits and Desirables, measuring the solutions against them, assessing the risks, and making refinements.

Limits:

Not cost any more to produce.

Desirables:

1. Be more space effective.
2. Be more stable on passenger tray tables.
3. Be easier to handle and store.
4. Optimize market exposure.
5. Be marketable to other clients.
6. Be acceptable to TransAmerican passengers.

Each of the four semifinal solutions needs to be evaluated against each criteria. Then the risks must be calculated, and, if necessary, the solution refined. Let's take them one at a time.

Solution

Short, squat individual-sized bottles, stored end-to-end in foam boxes

Limits:	
Not cost any more to produce	Same cost

Desirables:	
More space-effective	Space-saving styrofoam, bottles stored end-to-end
More stable on trays	Add weight to bottom of bottle
Easy to handle, store	Doesn't solve loading problem
Market exposure	Each passenger has bottle with our label
Other clients	Should appeal to other clients
Acceptable to passengers	Passengers likely to accept

Risk

If... passengers object to unfamiliar shape of bottle,
Then... they won't buy the wine.

Refined Solution

Design an attractive, eye-catching bottle and label for the shorter, individual-sized bottles; add weight to bottom of bottles; pack end-to-end in styrofoam.

Solution	
Full-sized bottles, attendant pours individual glasses	
Limits: Not cost any more to produce	Same cost
Desirables: More space-effective	Doesn't solve space problem
More stable on trays	Won't be on trays
Easy to handle, store	Doesn't solve loading problem
Market exposure	Passengers won't see label
Other clients	Marginal
Acceptable to passengers	Marginal

Risk

If... attendants are subject to extra work,
Then... they won't promote the wine.

Refined Solution

Ask attendant to serve first glass of wine. Provide bar in front of cabin for refills and advertise wine in airline's in-flight magazine.

Solution	
Individual cardboard containers with vacuum-packed foil interiors	
Limits: Not cost any more to produce	Vacuum packing increases cost (violates limit—no further evaluation needed for this solution)
Desirables: More space-effective More stable on trays Easy to handle, store Market exposure Other clients Acceptable to passengers	
Risk	
Refined Solution	

Solution	
Plastic cups sealed in foil	
Limits:	
Not cost any more to produce	Same cost
Desirables:	
More space-effective	More space-efficient
More stable on trays	Won't tip as easily, but wine could splash out
Easy to handle, store	Plastic lighter than glass; easier to store
Market exposure	Put label on cup
Other clients	Clients want wine in bottles
Acceptable to passengers	Probably not; perception that wine will not taste as good

Risk

If... passengers believe wine doesn't taste as good,
Then... they won't buy the wine; our image will be harmed.

Refined Solution

Produce wine cup under another label to protect image, but would negate market exposure.

The Final Culling

Once we've weighed each potential solution against each criterion, the best alternative should emerge clearly. In the case of Mistachio, the individualized cardboard containers solution was quickly eliminated because it didn't meet the cost Limit. The wine-in-cups solution, although viable, was eliminated because the wine would taste different, or be perceived as tasting different, than the bottled wine. You could market the "wine cup" under another label, but that would cancel out the Mistachio market exposure to the airline passengers. The solutions calling for shorter, individual-sized bottles or full-sized bottles poured by the attendants were refined to make them acceptable to Mistachio and to TransAmerican.

And the winner is… ?

Solution No. 1. The best solution is the shorter, squat individual-sized bottles. This meets every criteria, except it may not reduce the loading problem. The only foreseeable risk is that passengers won't like the new shape, but that hurdle can be minimized by making sure you come up with a good design.

By contrast, the other remaining option—asking attendants to pour from a large bottle—intrudes on TransAmerican's turf by making more demands of their employees. It also doesn't solve the loading problem, and is only marginally satisfactory in terms of market exposure and passenger acceptability. Furthermore, human nature being what it is, the attendants, being saddled by Mistachio with a new chore, probably won't knock themselves out to promote further wine sales. The refined solution of providing a bar in front of the cabin and increasing Mistachio advertising in the in-flight magazine is complicated, problematic, and perhaps more costly.

A Hands-Down Choice

All in all, then, it's a hands-down choice: Design an attractive shorter, individual-sized bottle, weighted on the bottom, and packed end-to-end in foam.

Just a short while ago, you had a difficult situation with a major client—and no alternatives in sight. But now you can go into that next meeting with TransAmerican confident that you've got a feasible, workable, low-risk solution.

That's Innovation!

Leveraging

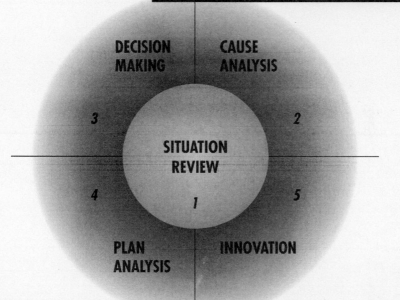

DECISION MAKING

CAUSE ANALYSIS

3

2

SITUATION REVIEW

1

4

5

PLAN ANALYSIS

INNOVATION

Now that you're well grounded in the thinking skills, you'll learn in the following three chapters ways to leverage this new knowledge. You'll see how thinking objectively can make you a more effective advocate for your own ideas. You'll find out how to best teach the thinking skills to others, thus helping yourself, the people you care most about, and your organization for years to come.

And, last but hardly least, you'll learn how people problems, so pervasive but so different from traditional problems, can also be analyzed fully and thoroughly and can be dealt with accurately and efficiently.

Chapter **Six**

Advocating
Getting Your Ideas Moving

Rebecca Smith's big breakthrough wasn't high drama. Instead, it came as she quietly munched on a pastrami on rye in the company cafeteria. Flipping through a clothing catalog, she saw a picture of a young boy, not unlike her son, clad in spiffy checks and denims sitting at a school desk.

Then the inspiration struck her! She saw it as clearly as if it already existed: the concept, the process, the product, the marketing—even the packaging.

Rebecca, a senior programmer at MacroTek, suddenly and fully understood that by just a relatively simple reworking of its award-winning business software, Macrotek could launch an educational line that was almost sure to be a winner. Instead of just helping CPAs with their spreadsheets and actuarials with their probabilities, "Accu-Biz" could become "Accu-Math" and could help grade-schoolers with their arithmetic, high school kids with their algebra and calculus, and college students with their statistics and economics. It could vastly accelerate the learning curve and, perhaps more important, "Accu-Math" could—with some graphics twists—make any kind of math challenge truly *fun!*

Generations of anxiety could be laid to rest. Students would be amazed, teachers relieved, and parents pleased. And Macrotek would be overjoyed at the chance to open a vast new market and increase sagging profit margins.

Rebecca was thrilled. Never in her career had she felt as jazzed about an idea. She *knew*—as she knew few other things with certainty—that she was onto something. Her only question was *What do I do now?*

Build a better mousetrap, and the world will beat a path to your door. That's the old saying. But it's never been accurate, and it's even less true today. You must be able to get your ideas recognized, sold, and acted upon. In this chapter, we'll look at how to get ideas broad-based support and a kick in the pants. Such a kick is needed because it's not enough to just come up with a new concept. No idea, however great, gets anywhere unless it's adopted by an organization. And there's a lot of resistance in most organizations to saying "yes"—even if the idea is workable. More important than an idea's workability per se is whether it has support from those who can make it happen. The set of skills used to win that support is called *advocating*.

Rebecca finished her sandwich and went back to her cubicle still brimming with excitement about her idea. She even fantasized a bit, wondering if the company might name a new wing in their building needed to house the new operation after her or give her a big bonus, a larger office, or at least some special recognition. She thought maybe she should go immediately to see the head of Research and Development, or even to the company president. But then reality set in, and she said to herself, *Wait a minute!*

Are they going to be as thrilled as I am? Are they going to give me credit? Or are they going to scoff at a potentially multimillion dollar idea coming from a mere programmer? Is it somehow going to look bad for them that *I* came up with this instead of them?

Rebecca sighed. She hoped not. But, on the other hand, she had been politically stung a time or two in her 13 years at Macrotek.

Maybe, she reflected, she ought to think about this for a while before she plunged in headfirst.

All ideas need support if they're going to be implemented. What kind of support? Many kinds, possibly including funding, staff, space, time, equipment, or simply an official sign-off. An idea's brilliance doesn't guarantee support, nor does its technological or economic worth. Instead, gaining support requires a carefully worked out and well-executed advocacy strategy.

Almost any organization erects barriers to change:

- **Change is destabilizing.** It can conflict with the organization's desire for control and predictability.

- **Change usually requires approval by a variety of people.** Those people often have different needs and interests.

- **Supporting change means taking risks.** Many people have a harder time supporting an approach that *might* work rather than one that *has* worked in the past.

Recognizing these roadblocks is the first step in figuring out ways around them. Understand, though, that there's not something necessarily sinister at work here. It's not that firms, organizations, or most individuals delight in blocking fresh ideas. It's just that they set up wonderful systems to handle the flow of production, people, and paperwork so that things will get done on time and by certain people in a certain way. Those same systems make change difficult.

A simple illustration: Production may rightly think it has its hands full making Macrotek's line of business software. It's not hard to see how that department might view Rebecca's new idea not as a wondrous educational breakthrough, but as another chore it's going to have to accomplish—and perhaps accomplish without additional resources. Especially if Production feels left out of the decision to go ahead, it might dig in its heels.

So while everyone involved in judging an idea may be competent and right minded, they often have competing interests. Yet, to make a change, cooperation must be gained from everyone affected. That's not easy.

There's No Place Like Home

Rebecca's not a rookie. She knows that few probably are going to be as interested in seeing her idea succeed as she is. She knows that organizations, like the people who run them, aren't totally logical. For starters, innovations are often improvements in the way things are done—in her case, producing a new product for a possible new market. Any suggestion of improvement implies that the current system isn't working as well as it should. So some people, feeling threatened, may take issue with that implication, regardless of the rightness of Rebecca's idea or its potential benefit to the company.

To make it worse, Rebecca isn't an executive, isn't paid to be a strategic thinker. Her idea potentially could rile some who are. That's because Macrotek, like most companies, talks a lot about encouraging ideas from the rank and file, but, in fact, such ideas can pose dangers to higher-ups who may have to concede they hadn't thought of this. Rebecca remembered a quote from one of her college professors: "Neutrality is a luxury enjoyed only by those whose interests are not threatened." He was talking about foreign relations, but it sometime seemed equally apt for corporate relations.

For instance, Rebecca is aware that people between her and the Major Decision Maker may try to protect themselves or their bosses by denying her support. And the Major Decision Maker may not see what's going on because he or she is too busy looking at the big picture.

The more Rebecca thinks about it, the more certain she is that she must take the time to develop her idea and carefully plan a campaign for support. If "Accu-Math" is to become reality, she is going to need to influence Macrotek's decision-making processes.

One-hour film processing. Customer-service hotlines. Laptop computers. Bar codes. Outplacement counseling. Employee involvement groups. Microwave popcorn. Drive-up banking. All are products or concepts now accepted as standard practices. But once they were mere ideas in need of advocacy.

New and useful ideas can be products (stick-on notes) or processes (computer bulletin boards). They can be internal to a department, division, or firm; or they can directly affect customers. They don't have to be original: They can be new to you, but not unique in the world. Or they can be pieces of several other ideas spliced together to fill your need. Whatever your idea is, if it's to stand a good chance of being implemented, it requires advocacy. The best advocates, in fact, continuously weave organizational support into their ideas as they develop and plan them.

To do that, they follow these four steps:

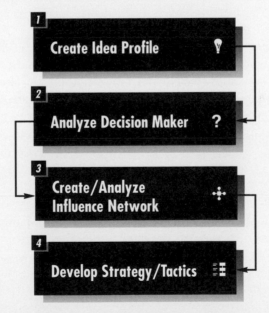

Successful leaders are experienced and savvy in using the advocacy process. Most of them understand it intuitively and employ it automatically when they have an idea to sell.

Even CEOs may use this process within their own organization. In that case, the Decision Maker would be some key employee—or group of employees—whose support the CEO needs to ensure a project's success.

STEP ONE

Create Idea Profile

Rebecca Smith thinks she has a great idea, one that could profit the company, help thousands of customers, and maybe boost her career. But she's savvy enough to know that virtue alone will not sell an idea internally. She first must do an Idea Profile. That will describe the opportunity, the idea, and what it will take to get the idea developed. This step will also pinpoint the crucial decision that could either ensure or block success. First, she should describe the opportunity her idea would exploit. What need, problem, or goal inspired the idea? How could she describe her idea briefly to someone else in the organization?

Then she should figure out what will be needed to put the idea into effect. For example, she will want to think about who will need to provide what information, resources, or approvals to move the idea along. She will want to ponder the potential problems and how she will seek to prevent or minimize them. She will also want to think specifically about how to gain support and where, when, and how she can eventually test her idea.

An important point: In the life of every idea, there is a Checkmate Decision. This is a major pivot point, a make-or-break action that either assures that your plan can proceed or that effectively side-tracks or kills it. It's a key part of the Idea Profile. Finding that Checkmate Decision can be challenging because it can vary with every idea and every organization; it is often as much of a political decision as a practical one. But you need to identify this decision, the Major Decision Maker, and a deadline date for approval.

Rebecca works on her Idea Profile, trying to figure out what needs to happen before Macrotek can move forward on designing and developing her educational-software line. Her list of needs looks like this:

- Allocate space for project planning.
- Have Sam Jones assigned as project leader.

- Get five technicians assigned to the team.
- Obtain some initial funding.
- Finish first design in four months.

That's a bare-bones development plan. But Rebecca thinks it's probably the most she can hope for in these uncertain economic times. She thinks Macrotek would need to have the preliminary design in hand within four months because its aggressive competitors may hear about the project and try to beat Macrotek to the punch. She thinks the team could turn out the design faster if it were given more technicians or more money, but that's not likely.

Next, she ponders the question, Which of those is the Checkmate Decision? Which step, if blocked, could kill the effort? She decides it's getting Sam Jones named as project leader. He's the assistant R&D manager—young, connected, respected, and supremely capable. Besides, he's more open to new ideas than his boss, Charley Hankins, head of R&D. To Rebecca, Charley seems wedded to the old product line, which he helped develop over the past 10 years. His pride of authorship may limit his vision. Some of Rebecca's other criteria—the space, for example, or the number of techs—could fail to be fully met, and the project could still succeed. That's because Sam, a tenacious leader, would find a way around those problems. But without Sam, she is sure the project wouldn't have the horsepower to succeed. So she needs to get Sam chosen—and soon. But with Charley Hankins in the top spot at R&D, that's not going to be easy. Only Mr. Hargrove, the senior vice president for Operations, is likely to be able to override Charley and anoint Sam. And if Rebecca is to meet her deadline, Hargrove needs to make that decision within a month.

STEP TWO

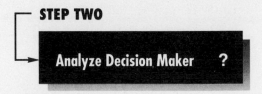

Analyze Decision Maker   ?

Okay, Rebecca has her idea and knows what it's going to take for implementation. She's pinpointed the Checkmate Decision (appointment of Sam Jones) and the Major Decision Maker (Mr. Hargrove).

The next task is to analyze the Major Decision Maker. What's the best way to approach the Major Decision Maker? To know that, you must understand a good deal about this person. This takes some thought and maybe some research, too. First, what are the Major Decision Maker's *primary interests* as they relate to your idea? These interests can be of two broad kinds: personal and organizational.

- **Personal.** What's he like? Is he a risk taker, a maverick, or a devout middle-of-the-roader? Does he see himself as a pioneer, a trailblazer? Or as an orthodox corporate soul who'll get ahead by diligence and obedience rather than daring and brilliance? Is he secure enough in his own position that he won't feel threatened by you and your idea?

- **Organizational.** Does he make big decisions on his own? Does he have a strong interest in new ventures? What part of the business most excites him: production, sales, service, administration? Does he have the clout to really get things done?

Second, what risks will the Decision Maker likely see in your idea? What, from his standpoint, might go wrong? Maybe he's been burned when he backed another idea like yours. Or perhaps he's on shaky ground with his boss and thus is being particularly cautious now.

Third, what will the Decision Maker's likely position be on your idea? Positive? Negative? Neutral? Unknown?

And last, what's his style of decision making? This can affect the way data is perceived or whether it's perceived at all. Knowing this will help you decide what information you need and in what form. For example, some people make decisions based not so much on facts as on feelings. Hunches, intuition, and how they feel about certain people account for more than, say, statistical analysis. So you wouldn't want to go to that person with an inch-thick report filled with graphs and pie charts. You'd probably want your presentation to be more anecdotal, more subjective. For other leaders, though, that might be precisely the wrong prescription. They may prefer to make decisions based on study of the best, fullest, and most recent information. They might be interested more in the logic of the decision than in your feelings or even their own feelings about it. There are four basic decision-making styles:

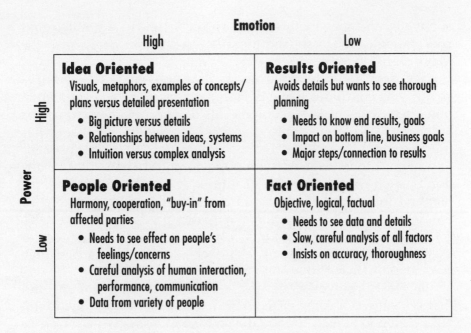

Emotion

	High	Low
High	**Idea Oriented** Visuals, metaphors, examples of concepts/plans versus detailed presentation • Big picture versus details • Relationships between ideas, systems • Intuition versus complex analysis	**Results Oriented** Avoids details but wants to see thorough planning • Needs to know end results, goals • Impact on bottom line, business goals • Major steps/connection to results
Low	**People Oriented** Harmony, cooperation, "buy-in" from affected parties • Needs to see effect on people's feelings/concerns • Careful analysis of human interaction, performance, communication • Data from variety of people	**Fact Oriented** Objective, logical, factual • Needs to see data and details • Slow, careful analysis of all factors • Insists on accuracy, thoroughness

(row labels, left margin: "Power" spanning "High" and "Low")

Rebecca thinks about how to approach Mr. Hargrove, her Major Decision Maker. She first thinks perhaps she should make a frontal attack: Simply go to him, present her case, and ask for an OK.

But, then, she has second thoughts. For starters, Rebecca doesn't have direct access to Mr. Hargrove; even if she did, she doesn't believe she's likely to have much influence over him. He's never gone out of his way to be particularly friendly to her. He's not been unkind; they just lack rapport. To her, he seems aloof and distant. Also, she thinks, Mr. Hargrove probably will need information from others, or want preliminary decisions from others, before he'll be willing to risk Charley Hankins's wrath by appointing Sam Jones project leader.

Maybe he'll think her idea is too far afield for Macrotek or involves too many competitive risks. Even more likely, Rebecca notes, is that Mr. Hargrove may not want to pull Sam Jones off a project he's already assigned to, a project that Mr. Hargrove has high hopes for. All of these concerns cause Rebecca to be cautious about how she goes about seeking approval. She wants to be smart and strategic. To do so, she must begin with an analysis of the Major Decision Maker.

She does some thinking about him and queries others discreetly. She concludes that Mr. Hargrove carefully analyzes situations before he makes decisions. He'll take risks—and has the authority to do so—but only after he's satisfied himself that he has fully explored the upsides and the downsides. Mr. Hargrove likes to do things in increments, with opportunities to bail out if results don't match expectations. This cautious style has worked well for him and for Macrotek. He, as much as anyone, is responsible for the company's solid reputation as a quality producer. If Macrotek's software line is considered in the industry to be a bit stodgy, at least the firm hasn't gone off half-cocked, taking big speculative risks that it then has to abort at great cost.

So Mr. Hargrove has never presided over a huge failure, and that is a source of some pride to him. One other thing: She found out he's a good delegator and doesn't recoil from giving power or credit to those below him. Rebecca sums up the situation with Mr. Hargrove this way:

- **Primary interest:** Backing winners. As a confidant put it, "He'd rather have a high batting average than hit a lot of home runs. His reputation in the company and in the industry for consistency is very important to him.

- **Perceived risks:** It will be a costly start-up in a new field. And it will pull Sam Jones away from a "sure thing" project he's already working on.

- **Likely position:** Neutral. But may become positive *if* she can show him that the potential benefits far outweigh the risks and that there will be chances to cancel or scale back the project once it's under way.

- **Decision style:** Low power, low emotion. He'll want lots of hard facts.

Having analyzed the Major Decision Maker, you next should decide how you're going to approach him or her. The choices essentially are direct top-down, indirect bottom-up, or indirect-selective.

If the Decision Maker's likely position is favorable, if his primary interests align with your idea's benefits, if he perceives slight risk, and if his style matches the type of idea and plan you have, you probably can use a direct top-down strategy if the political environment in your organization would allow this approach. In this case, you'd just go directly to the Decision Maker for approval for your Checkmate Decision. The Decision Maker in all likelihood will approve it, and he'll see that everyone else supports it. However, it's usually not that simple. One doesn't often see such a favorable lineup of factors. Usually you will need to use one of the two indirect strategies.

The indirect bottom-up strategy means building grass-roots support at the lower levels of the organization where people will see the most benefits. This can be time-consuming and frustrating. But sometimes your idea is so risky to those who must approve it—maybe because of its enormous cost—that this is the only viable strategy. An indirect-selective strategy, on the other hand, entails building a cumulative case for your idea by finding allies at various levels and in various parts of the organization. Rebecca concludes that the indirect-selective approach is best for her situation.

STEP THREE

Create/Analyze Influence Network

Your Major Decision Maker probably listens to key people in the firm before making major, risky decisions. They may be his peers, his superiors, or even subordinates he has extraordinary trust in. These people constitute an Influence Network. Regardless of whether these people support or object to your idea, you can't ignore them. Who are they? Some categories appear below.

Resource allocators. These employees can provide or withhold budget, people, space, equipment, or services. Because everyone needs them, they often carry more clout than their title or salary suggests. Would they have something to gain or lose if your project moves ahead?

Experts. Who has knowledge of similar projects? Who has credibility in the area of your idea and might be listened to by your Major Decision Maker? Perhaps it's an outside consultant who's done similar work. Or maybe it's someone in another department who tried a similar project a year or so ago.

Opinion leaders. These are savvy, connected people whose knowledge, longevity, or relationships often give them an influence disproportionate to their spot on the flowchart. As "insiders," they often seem to know what's going on in the organization, have a finger on its pulse, and can sometimes predict reactions before they occur.

End users. These are people whose jobs or status may change because of your idea. They're sure to have an opinion or concern and can give you crucial feedback.

Personal influencers. The Decision Maker probably also has a personal advisor or two. These would be people with whom he has special rapport, whose judgment and discretion he trusts. They may not be highly placed in the chain of command. Finding them is no easy task, and influencing them may be equally difficult. But because of their possible sway over the Major Decision Maker, their help could be critical.

Rebecca makes some discreet inquiries. She finds that Mr. Hargrove, her Major Decision Maker, regularly plays golf in a foursome with Charley Hankins, Sam Jones, and an outside consultant named Ridgeway.

In fact, Hargrove brought Ridgeway in a few years ago to advise the firm on another start-up idea that he eventually recommended against. Ridgeway, considered almost a member of the "family," has Hargrove's ear. In terms of resource allocators, Rebecca thinks that the Administrative Services guy who parcels out the floor space and equipment probably should be on her list. His enthusiasm, or lack of, for making some square footage and material available could play a role. Experts, other than Charley

Hankins, seem to be in short supply. The company doesn't have many folks knowledgeable about educational software, precisely because it hasn't done much in that area.

As far as opinion leaders at Macrotek, the only one Rebecca can think of is Willard Wiley, the crusty, old chief accountant. He's never been made CFO because he's widely perceived as not being quite cut from upper-management cloth. But he's been crunching numbers at Macrotek since it was run out of a garage. His coarsely delivered views are an institution around the company, and people listen.

Among those end users directly affected are, first, Sam Jones and the five technicians who will be asked to serve on the project. Beyond them, the Production and Marketing departments surely would be involved. So Rebecca thinks she ought to include at least a key representative of each of them. As far as personal influencers, Rebecca learns that Mr. Hargrove has a close working relationship with Diane Wiggins, his highly able executive assistant. Diane is a progressive who's been known to encourage Mr. Hargrove to take more risks. She's also a feminist who thinks women should have more say in the company. That's a trump card Rebecca may want to play. And lest she forget, there's Charley Hankins, the R&D boss. He's probably her biggest concern. It's his ox that gets gored if Sam Jones, who works for him, is pulled away to work on Rebecca's project. Rebecca draws up a list:

Macrotek Influence Network

- Mr. Hargrove, senior vice president, Operations.
- Charley Hankins, R&D manager.
- Sam Jones, assistant R&D manager.
- Ridgeway, outside consultant.
- Administrative Services head.
- Willard Wiley, chief accountant.
- Technicians.
- Production head.
- Marketing head.
- Diane Wiggins, Hargrove's executive assistant.

Analyze Influence Network

Having identified the members of the Influence Network, you next need to figure out how they can help sell your idea. Where do they stand? How can you best appeal to them?

To answer these questions, try to put yourself in the Major Decision Maker's shoes and imagine what he or she might want to know before making the Checkmate Decision.

- What potential contributions might these persons provide about the Checkmate Decision (information, action)?

- What are their interests (personal and organizational) that might relate to your idea?

- What risks will they see in your idea? (What could go wrong? How could it interfere with their own success?)

- What will that person's likely position be on your idea (positive, negative, neutral, or unknown)?

- What is his or her Decision Style (idea oriented, results oriented, fact oriented, people oriented)?

All of this information will be used to create your Advocacy Strategy. It will tell you whom to contact and when, what outcome to expect from each, and the best way to gain their support.

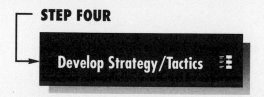

STEP FOUR

Develop Strategy/Tactics

The final planning step is creating a game plan for contacting those in the Influence Network. You'll need Strategy (the sequence you'll follow) and Tactics (what you will say and how you will say it). Timing, as they say, is everything. And with idea advocacy, that's doubly true. How long you will want to keep your idea quiet will depend on the degree to which your idea is likely to initially appeal to the organization. Almost any new idea will have natural enemies. And if it's a bold, high-risk idea—like Rebecca's—you could kill it if you tell too many people about it before you've gained support. Most successful advocates quietly develop their ideas and plan while gaining a broad base of support.

In fact, you may want to get a tacit understanding from those you contact that they'll issue approvals after you've begun talking about the idea openly. And, of course, the pilot test and implementation will only come after final approvals are given.

So, deciding for now to remain low-key, you create your strategy. You must first decide in what order you will contact people and what outcome you can expect. These guidelines may be helpful:

1. First, contact people who will strongly support your idea and can influence others by supplying resources, data, or clout.

2. Next, contact those who will likely support you based on approval of, or information from the people in the first step.

3. Then, contact neutral people who will support you based on the number of supporters you've already gained.

4. Finally, contact the people you need for information, action, or decisions before you can go to the Major Decision Maker, *who may oppose you*. Be sure you have lots of supportive data and a well-developed plan. Don't hesitate to throw names around at this point. Map out this strategy by listing in order—and by date—the names you'll contact. Start backwards from the time you need the Checkmate Decision. You will be able to contact some people more or less concurrently, while others will need information or evidence of others' support before you can go to them.

Rebecca studies the Influence Network list and does some figuring. She thinks the Checkmate Decision must be reached in a month, so she starts with that date, October 1, and works back, listing those contacts she'll want to make first.

Advocacy Strategy

Sept. 1:   Sam Jones. Outcome: positive.

Sept. 3:   Diane Wiggins. Outcome: neutral/positive.

Sept. 5: Technicians. Outcome: positive.
Sept. 10: Williard Wiley. Outcome: neutral/positive.
Sept. 12: Marketing head. Outcome: positive.
Sept. 13: Ridgeway. Outcome: unknown.
Sept. 14: Administrative Services head. Outcome: neutral.
Sept. 16: Production head. Outcome: negative.
Sept. 20: Charley Hankins, R&D manager. Outcome: negative.
Sept. 23: Mr. Hargrove, senior vice president/Operations. Outcome: unknown.

Create Advocacy Tactics

Once you've got your strategy, you'll need to develop tactics for approaching each person. In other words, what will you say and how will you say it?

Here are some steps:

- **Identify the benefits.** Which benefits of your idea will appeal to this person based on their primary interests and Decision Style?

- **Manage the risks.** How can you minimize potential risks? For example, if this person is likely to question the market for your idea, do you have research pointing to the probability of commercial success? Similarly, if this person is likely to be uncomfortable with making a risky decision, list the many supporters of your idea or mention other firms that have dealt successfully with similar risks.

- **Select a contact mode.** Should you call them, send a memo, arrange an appointment, or catch them informally near the drinking fountain? Think about their level in the organization (if they're two or more levels above you, you may want to contact them through your boss), their function (do engineers prefer to communicate differently than human-resources people?), and their Decision Style (a Results-Oriented person might prefer a brief memo, while an Idea-Oriented person likely would want personal conversation).

- **Choose appropriate materials.** Again, Decision Style can be a good guide here when deciding whether to prepare a detailed report, a prototype, or perhaps just point to other people who have experienced something like your idea.

As Rebecca details her tactics, the key question she asks herself is this: What actions can I take to ensure the expected outcome from each contact? Her list now looks like this:

Sept. 1: Sam Jones. Outcome: positive
- **Benefit:** Sam will like her idea and will quickly see how it'll be a big boost to him as well as to the company.
- **Risk:** He might be so involved in his present project that he wouldn't wish to switch.
- **Mode:** Sam's a very outgoing guy, so she thinks she should just approach him directly, but perhaps away from Charley Hankins. Rebecca will also ask Sam what five techs he would choose when, and if, the project is approved.
- **Materials:** Just enthusiasm for the idea.

Sept. 3: Diane Wiggins. Outcome: neutral/positive
- **Benefit:** She'll probably like the idea of the company taking a bit of a risk. The fact that a woman came up with the idea will likely appeal to her.
- **Risk:** Probably not much.
- **Mode:** Rebecca wouldn't want to embarrass her by talking in the vicinity of Mr. Hargrove, so she'll probably quietly ask Diane to lunch.
- **Materials:** Diane is People Oriented, so Rebecca will stress the effect of the idea on customer's lives.

Sept. 5: Technicians. Outcome: positive
- **Benefits:** They'll benefit by being included in an exciting new project.

- **Risk:** Not much from their standpoint.
- **Mode:** Individual, informal chats around the office. Rebecca will tell the technicians she's already talked to Sam Jones, and that will inspire them.
- **Materials:** Gather stories about the fun and *esprit de corps* enjoyed by technicians associated with other start-up projects.

Sept. 10: Willard Wiley, chief accountant. Outcome: neutral/positive
- **Benefit:** He'll like being consulted as a "player." If she can show him that Sam, Diane, and the techs are on board and demonstrate how the idea can result in a financial shot in the arm for the firm, Wiley can become a major ally. Rebecca also hopes to learn from him more about Ridgeway, the consultant.
- **Risk:** He would object to an excessive financial risk.
- **Mode:** An appointment in his office.
- **Materials:** As much hard data and reasoned argument as she can put together showing a bottom-line payoff. He's Results Oriented, so she'll want to be brief and to the point, stressing facts, not just dreams.

Sept. 12: Marketing chief. Outcome: positive
- **Benefit:** He'll welcome the chance to get a new, exciting product to sell, something the competition can't match.
- **Risk:** If the product doesn't sell, Marketing could take the heat.
- **Mode:** Appointment in his office.
- **Materials:** He's Idea Oriented. So he's going to prefer an upbeat, personalized briefing rather than a detailed report.

Sept. 13: Ridgeway, the consultant. Outcome: unknown
- **Benefit:** He might be hired to help in preparing for the launch of the new product.
- **Risk:** Might not feel sense of authorship; may resent her.

- **Mode:** Appointment outside the office.
- **Materials:** Don't know enough yet about his Decision Style. May know more after talking to Wiley on Sept. 10.

Sept. 14: Administrative Services head. Outcome: neutral

- **Benefit:** He's probably not going to care a lot about the idea except as it helps the company financially. Rebecca knows that most leaders present the Administrative chief with a fait accompli: They demand space after a project has been OK'd. She's expecting that working with him before approval is won will not only make him more excited about the project, but may result in a better space and better equipment.
- **Risk:** None, except added work.
- **Mode:** Phone call or informal meeting.
- **Materials:** Statistics on the size of the potential market.

Sept. 16: Production chief. Outcome: negative

- **Benefit:** Only the possible improvement in company's profitability.
- **Risk:** More work without more resources or recognition.
- **Mode:** Appointment in his office.
- **Materials:** As much detail as she can muster on the manufacturing process and how the additional effort won't be a hardship.

Sept. 20: Charley Hankins, R&D manager. Outcome: negative

- **Benefit:** R&D could look good if new product is a winner.
- **Risk:** Authority eroded. Will pull Sam Jones away from "sure thing" and take Macrotek in new direction that's scary.
- **Mode:** Appointment in his office.
- **Materials:** He's Fact Oriented and will require a full report with facts and figures. Rebecca plans to tell him how many others have already embraced the idea and that she's going to Mr. Hargrove.

Sept. 23: Mr. Hargrove, senior vice president/Operations. Outcome: unknown

- **Benefit:** He's going to recognize "Accu-Math" as potentially tapping a vast and growing market. It will be a chance to broaden Macrotek's product line, get a leg up on the competition, and bolster the firm's lagging profits.

- **Risk:** A mistake would damage his image.

- **Mode:** Ask Diane Wiggins or Ridgeway to set up an appointment. Clear it with her own boss. Maybe Sam Jones or Ridgeway would also put in a word with Mr. Hargrove about the importance of listening to Rebecca's proposal.

- **Materials:** He's Fact Oriented and risk averse, so he'll want a full, detailed report. Mention all endorsements and be sure to include fail-safe checkpoints in the plan so he could jettison the project if results falter.

Capturing the support of others may sound like a lot of work. It *is*. But there's also a lot at stake. And a successful advocacy can provide a payoff that's worth many times the effort expended.

Successful idea generators must be committed, practically willing to run through a brick wall to get their idea sold. They need to be able to identify the principal players and know how and when to present the proposal.

Again, here are the four steps they should follow:

1. Create an Idea Profile.
2. Analyze the Major Decision Maker.
3. Create and Analyze the Influence Network.
4. Develop an Advocacy Strategy and Tactics.

Rebecca is now almost ready for her big meeting on September 23 with Mr. Hargrove. A lot will be riding on that encounter. So she wisely concludes that she needs to surmount one last hurdle: brushing up on her presentation skills.

She's confident about her idea and her research into the Influence Network. It's her sales skills she wonders about. She doesn't make these kinds of presentations often. In addition, she doesn't know Mr. Hargrove well and often finds him distant. So she needs to do what she can to become relaxed, engaging, and persuasive.

She decides to talk to her friend and associate Sam Jones. He's an accomplished presenter, respected not only for the information he imparts, but the interesting yet factual way he does it. He'll give her some pointers.

The ability to persuade is probably the single most common trait among successful people. And, of course, it's a linchpin of the advocacy process. You can be the best idea generator on the continent, but if you can't persuade others, your ideas will remain orphans.

Here are some key points to remember in preparing the content of any presentation:

1. **Know the history.** Know the answer to the question, What decisions have been made in the past with respect to the alternative I'm presenting? You don't want to spin your wheels and waste your boss's time on ideas that already have been fully considered and rejected . . . or, for that matter, fully considered, approved, and about to be implemented. For example, you wouldn't want to be trying to sell the CEO on why top executives should, or shouldn't, be flying first-class on commercial airliners when the company has already decided to buy its own plane.

2. **Know the needs of the person or group you're selling to.** How will your idea help others and the organization as well as yourself? Your earlier analysis of the Major Decision Maker and your creation of advocacy tactics should be helpful here. Essentially, what you're trying to do is discover the relevant criteria and then see how you can present your option in a way that will make it rank higher than any other option under consideration.

3. **Be prepared to minimize the risks involved.** Again, you already know what the Major Decision Maker may see as a risk. Be prepared to offer Preventive Actions and Contingent Actions (such as was shown in Plan Analysis) to minimize any remaining fear on the part of the Major Decision Maker.

4. **Minimize any perceived threat.** An idea presented in a way that makes the advocate a winner and someone else a loser probably isn't going to fly. And it may do the advocate more harm than good in the long run. Presenters need to ask some "How will...?" questions before broaching their idea. For example, How will this idea affect my boss? My peers? My subordinates, and, of course, How will it affect the organization?

As you can see, the format of your presentation parallels that of the Decision Making skill. After all, what you're trying to do is get the Major Decision Maker to make a favorable decision about your proposal. If you and the Major Decision Maker both are well grounded in the thinking skills, the process should be that much easier because you'll have a common language and a similar mindset during each step of the presentation.

Now sure of the content, an advocate next needs to prepare for the style of the presentation. There are six basic points to keep in mind:

1. **Try to be yourself.** Most people fail as presenters when they try to be something they are not. They come across as artificial, and that detracts from the message.

2. **Be confident.** This is probably the most important part of any presentation. If you're not self-assured, the audience will sense it, and your idea will suffer.

3. **Use extended eye contact.** Look directly into the eyes of as many people as you can for about four to five seconds each during your presentation.

4. **Gesture and speak naturally.** Try to be loose and relaxed. Some people pretend they're at a social affair talking to one of their close friends. If you're excited about what you're presenting, using natural gestures usually comes automatically. Likewise, try not to talk too slow, too fast, or in a monotone, or to trail off at the end of a sentence. Again, being confident helps with both gestures and voice.

5. **Tell stories and use examples.** Audiences want and need concrete examples to help them understand. The more good examples, the more effective and interesting the presentation.

6. **Dress appropriately.** Being inappropriately attired can distract the audience from your idea. If in doubt, overdress; being formally attired at an informal gathering is far better than the reverse.

Rebecca, now that she's been briefed by Sam Jones on the nuts and bolts of making a presentation, is increasingly confident about her meeting with Mr. Hargrove. She knows the company has never considered an idea such as her educational software. She believes she's done enough research to know the needs of Mr. Hargrove (lots of facts leading to a surefire winner) and the needs of the firm (a strong but relatively safe addition to the bottom line).

Rebecca also is aware of what risks her idea may be perceived as carrying (a costly start-up in a new field), and she's going to address those head-on for Mr. Hargrove. Her idea likely will be seen by everyone as a threat to Charley Hankins, the head of R&D, and a boost to Sam Jones. So she'll need to be careful not to salt those wounds by gloating or dismissing the personal ramifications.

She's going to wear a conservative suit to her meeting with Mr. Hargrove, lace her presentation with examples and anecdotes told, as much as possible, in a loose, natural way, while maintaining eye contact and speaking confidently.

If she can do all that, Rebecca thinks she'll get a fair hearing and will have a good chance of seeing her Accu-Math idea endorsed. She hopes it is, for the company's sake primarily and, secondarily, for her own pride and success.

But even if Mr. Hargrove turns thumbs down, Rebecca will take solace in having been a strong advocate. She now knows the process. She knows her own analytical skills. She knows how to make a presentation. She even knows her company and its people better than she did just a short time ago.

When her next idea pops up, whether it's when she's bent over her work or over a pastrami on rye, she'll know exactly what to do.

Chapter **Seven**

The New Leader
*Developing the Thinking Skills
in Others*

"The cream will rise to the top," your mother may have told you encouragingly. Of course, she meant well, and she was right—to a degree. But like so many ancient aphorisms, that one can be misleading in today's business world. Yes, cream does naturally rise. And so do people with ability. But even the smallest dairy farmer knows that's a ridiculously inefficient and time-consuming way to make cream. Instead, the farmer speeds up the process by purchasing a separator to produce a predictable amount and quality of cream.

Similarly, the ability to think effectively may assert itself over the fullness of time. But leaders must hasten and refine the process. That requires understanding how people learn and then committing yourself to leading the learning process.

The Mandate to Teach

Remember that old saw about how if you give a man a fish, you feed him today—but teach him how to fish and you've fed him forever? Well, now that you know the five thinking skills, you're well on your way to being able to handle any situation.

But while being able to handle a certain situation will help you and your organization today, teaching those skills to others will help you both for decades to come. Any good leader thinks

137

long-term. And long-term, it's in everyone's interest to bring along the next generation of leaders.

Besides, it's buoying to help others put the thinking skills into action. Think how proud you would have been if Mark, our protagonist in the Situation Review scenario, worked for you at the bank or if you had been the one who'd taught Angela the Decision-Making skills needed to make her tough Chicago real estate choices. Think of the peace of mind you'd achieve as a leader, or even as a parent, if you knew your subordinates, or children, were thinking through their concerns clearly.

All managers, whether they acknowledge it not, whether it's in their job description or not, have this responsibility. It's a social contract with future generations if not with the current generation. Unfortunately, in too many cases, the task is handed off to human resources or management development specialists. Training specialists have their role, but the buck really stops with the manager on the line.

Teaching the thinking skills, though, isn't like teaching someone to use a computer or prepare a report. The thinking skills, as you know by now, are not tasks like how to interview job applicants or how to put together a three-year plan. The thinking skills do not entail an easily verifiable behavior. Instead, they have more to do with developing the power to analyze, learning patience and thoroughness, and increasing one's reasoning ability. However, they are *skills* that anyone can learn.

Formalizing Common Sense

You might say the thinking skills are a method for formalizing common sense. The thinking skills are not something you either have or you don't.

Rather, they involve transforming unconscious thinking into information processing. You won't find this under traditional classifications of leadership activity. To the contrary, the thinking skills encompass all leadership activity—not just certain levels, or certain times, or specific tasks.

While I wouldn't claim that the thinking skills can replace good instincts, I do know they can improve judgment. Because effective decision making is a combination of good data, well-reasoned alternatives, and adequate assessment of risks. The thinking skills ensure all of these are included in any decision.

The Learner as Golfer

Imagine for a moment that you're trying to teach golf to people who have never held a club before. You'd take them out on the links and, before you let them swing a club, you'd explain the fundamentals of the game. You might talk about the importance of the proper grip, the correct stance, and the function of each club. Then, once they'd demonstrated they understood all that, you'd have them show you what they could do.

They would probably flail away in a manner that would turn the groundskeeper's hair gray overnight. Divots would fly. Balls might careen off the tee at wild angles. Other golfers likely would duck for cover.

In short, your students would be in the first stage of the four-stage learning model:

- **Stage 1:** Unconscious Incompetence
- **Stage 2:** Conscious Incompetence
- **Stage 3:** Conscious Competence
- **Stage 4:** Unconscious Competence

Learning any skill involves passing through these four stages. If you, as a leader, understand them, you'll be a more effective teacher, and you'll help speed up your student's learning cycle. In many cultures around the world to be called a "teacher" is the greatest compliment a person can receive. As leaders we should all strive to be called "my teacher" by our subordinates.

While ignorance may be bliss to some, it's also a major stumbling block to learning. That's because students who aren't aware of the need to improve can't improve.

Now, with golf, it's pretty obvious when someone doesn't know what they're doing. But with more sophisticated business skills—say, performing a Cause Analysis—the visible effects are more subtle. And for you as a leader/teacher, your first job is to get the student up to Stage 2: Conscious Incompetence.

How do you do that? There's only one method: awareness. You must make students aware of what they don't know. They will furnish some of that through self-awareness. But one of your primary roles is to show them how much better they *could* be and then make sure they're aware of how they're measuring up to your expectations.

You'll need to define the skills and give the students a model. This is what Stage 1 is all about. Once they're aware of what they don't know and are willing to master the skill, they're ready to advance to Stage 2.

The Importance of Feedback

In Stage 2, the learner is trying to put his or her newfound knowledge into action. Your feedback becomes critical. But you must pick your spots and not overwhelm the learner. Too much feedback or feedback given in a negative way will turnoff the learner.

I'm sure all golf instructors have been tempted to say to every pupil they've ever had, "Perhaps you should take up a different sport." But, resist that! Instead, try to find something to praise, something he or she is close to doing well. This is important because you need to build on small successes to raise the learner's confidence.

Your feedback, while a key element, doesn't by itself produce learning. You can tell the aspiring golfer how important it is to keep his or her head still during the backswing and how to follow through after striking the ball. That likely will be helpful. But the main thing your feedback does is show the golfer that he or she needs to do better. Your feedback alone doesn't make the ball go straighter or farther—that's going to take practice. A *lot* of practice.

How do you give feedback on thinking skills? There are three methods. The first two—project review and skills checkoff—are formal. The last one is informal, and we'll discuss it later.

Project review means giving your student projects that require use of the thinking skills. Then you need to consciously monitor progress, providing feedback at key steps. With skills checkoff, you systematically assess the student's performance on all five thinking skills, pinpointing strengths and weaknesses at different times during a given period.

The following chart may help focus your feedback by showing your protégé how he or she is doing with the components of each of the thinking skills.

Scoring Directions Independently, a manager and direct report should assess the individual's current skill level and the importance of each process step using a 1–5 scale.

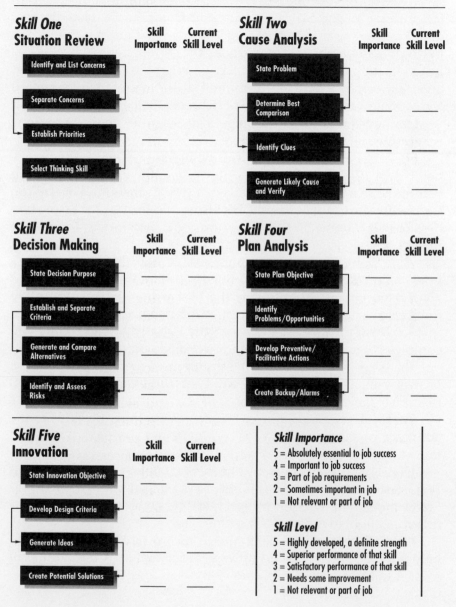

Skill One **Situation Review**	Skill Importance	Current Skill Level
Identify and List Concerns	——	——
Separate Concerns	——	——
Establish Priorities	——	——
Select Thinking Skill	——	——

Skill Two **Cause Analysis**	Skill Importance	Current Skill Level
State Problem	——	——
Determine Best Comparison	——	——
Identify Clues	——	——
Generate Likely Cause and Verify	——	——

Skill Three **Decision Making**	Skill Importance	Current Skill Level
State Decision Purpose	——	——
Establish and Separate Criteria	——	——
Generate and Compare Alternatives	——	——
Identify and Assess Risks	——	——

Skill Four **Plan Analysis**	Skill Importance	Current Skill Level
State Plan Objective	——	——
Identify Problems/Opportunities	——	——
Develop Preventive/Facilitative Actions	——	——
Create Backup/Alarms	——	——

Skill Five **Innovation**	Skill Importance	Current Skill Level
State Innovation Objective	——	——
Develop Design Criteria	——	——
Generate Ideas	——	——
Create Potential Solutions	——	——

Skill Importance
5 = Absolutely essential to job success
4 = Important to job success
3 = Part of job requirements
2 = Sometimes important in job
1 = Not relevant or part of job

Skill Level
5 = Highly developed, a definite strength
4 = Superior performance of that skill
3 = Satisfactory performance of that skill
2 = Needs some improvement
1 = Not relevant or part of job

Toward Stage 3

Whatever form your feedback takes, such dialogue can be helpful for pushing toward Stage 3: Conscious Competence. Here the student knows how to do something but requires time and thought to perform adequately. The golfer goes through a mental checklist as he or she prepares to tee off: hands gripping the club properly, feet a certain distance apart and pointed at the correct angle, and so forth. Stage 3 is the fragile state of the recently learned skill.

How does one get from Stage 2 to Stage 3? There's only one way: practice, practice, practice.

Figuring out how to train someone in thinking skills is more difficult than teaching a single, easily observable skill. It's easier to determine if a person, say, can drive a forklift than if he or she can do an effective Cause Analysis. It's also easier to gauge the effectiveness of that training by seeing, for example, how many accidents a forklift operator has before and after training. That's simpler than assessing how someone calibrates risk or how he or she gauges potential problems and opportunities in a Plan Analysis.

Asking process questions is the best way to make certain the novice stays at a state of Conscious Competence. Remember your first job? You probably knew very little initially, but each time you completed a task, someone would say, "Did you remember to...?"

That's certainly the way it was with me. Hired by Xerox Corp., I saw myself as a bright, young MBA graduate eager to bound into the upper ranks of management.

But I was *so* green. I had no training in the thinking skills or the advocacy process. I was always coming to my superiors with what I thought were "can't miss" ideas. But they almost always missed.

That's because my boss would ask me one or two process questions, such as "Have you thought of all the hidden expenses?" or "How much time will this project take? Remember, you still have a monthly quota to achieve!"

For a while, those kinds of questions brought me to a skidding halt. I had been so wrapped up in my idea that I hadn't thought of these additional issues. Obliquely, my boss was teaching me some of the thinking skills.

Eventually, I caught on. Then when I'd make a recommendation, I'd prepare my answers to the questions I *knew* he would ask. Without ever seeming to do so, he had taught me his thought processes. And I achieved Stage 3.

We do this all the time with our families, too. Remember as a teenager when you'd ask your folks for permission to do something out of the ordinary, say, spend a summer working in a national park? The questions would fly fast and furious in response: Where are you going to get the money? Who's going to help take care of your dog while you're gone? What effect will this have on our ability to pay for your college tuition?

Pretty soon you caught on. You learned that these grand ideas must be thought through, the risks and rewards considered, the alternatives outlined. So the next time you came to your mom or dad with such a request, you brought the answers to the predictable questions.

A Full Kit of Tools

When you know the thinking skills, you have a full set of tools with which to teach your subordinates, or for that matter your children. You know how to get them to think. And the way you do that is by making sure you ask the right questions.

The situations can vary immensely: The company president says he wants your department "totally revamped" within the next 90 days; your son or daughter doesn't have a clue about how or where to find a summer job; the IRS announces it's going to audit you next month; or Christmas is a week away and you haven't done a thing.

Each of these is an unwieldy, chaotic situation. So you know you'll want to ask the Situation Review questions:

- What are the concerns?
- How can you separate the concerns?
- What are the priorities?
- What skills should we use to resolve the concerns?

Or maybe the case is that something went wrong, and you don't know why. Let's say sales suddenly dropped 15 percent for no obvious reason. Or the soccer coach decided not to play your young son any more this season. Or the company president has stopped dropping by when he visits your region. Or maybe your spouse utters those sugary, but dreaded words, "Hon, did you gain some weight over the holidays, or did that outfit shrink?"

Whichever, you've got a Cause Analysis on your hands, and the questions to teach your underlings, your family, or, in the case of the added poundage, yourself, are as follows:

- What exactly has gone wrong?
- What are the "before"/"after" differences?
- What's changed?
- What's the most likely cause, and how can you verify it?

Or perhaps something just needs to get done. Maybe you've been thrust into the job market as a result of a downsizing. Or your daughter needs to decide which college to attend. Or your boss wants your proposal on a site and a theme for next year's national sales meeting. Or your boy's turning 16 and is itching to drive; you've got to decide whether he gets a car, how it and the insurance will be paid for, and what rules will accompany the privilege.

All involve decisions of some kind, so all call for Decision Making. These are the usual questions:

- What exactly are you deciding?
- What are the criteria?
- What options best satisfy the criteria?
- What could go wrong?

Or maybe your situation doesn't involve making a decision per se as much as ensuring that a decision already made turns out to be successful. For example, your boss creates an idea for a new product to add to your line, adding, "You figure out what needs to be done—*and just do it!*" Or your son solicits your help in getting him ready for football tryouts. Or your firm has just acquired a small competitor, and you're asked to make it a smooth marriage. Or even more literally, your daughter's acquiring a husband and asks your help in arranging a June wedding.

In short, you need to come up with a plan. You need to do a Plan Analysis by asking the following questions:

- What are the plan's critical areas or steps?
- What are the potential problems/opportunities?
- How can problems be prevented and opportunities seized?
- What could go wrong? How will we know? What will we do if it does?

Finally, your employees, or your family, may need help in creating new concepts: A competitor is beating you in every new market and you need something that will snap your firm's losing streak. A daughter is alone and unhappy at college because her friends have graduated or transferred. Your boss wants to know what it will take to make your company's telecommunication state-of-the-art. Your friend is a successful author but needs a breakthrough to put her on the best-seller list.

These situations call for Innovation. These are the questions you'd want to ask:

- What's the objective?
- What are the criteria you've got to meet?
- What are your new ideas?
- How can those ideas be mixed or matched into workable solutions?

Teaching through process questions is a simpler, less structured, and less formal way to teach the thinking skills. If you practice using these questions, you'll soon see your student achieve Stage 3: Conscious Competence—the goal of every teacher.

Achieving Stage 4: Unconscious Competence

For most of the skills we learn, the aim must be to reach Stage 4: Unconscious Competence, doing it right without even thinking about it. Training in any form, though, can't progress a person past Stage 3. The skill must be internalized.

This is the ultimate goal of all learning. It's an exciting state of performance. It's like the first time you ski a hill and enjoy it because you did it naturally rather than thoughtfully or the first time your tennis backhand flows easily because you didn't have to visualize it as a six-step movement.

Fourth-stage learners are free to concentrate on their goals rather than on their skills. Doing it properly becomes the expectation, not a big deal. Our golfer now swings cleanly, freely, smoothly without thinking about it. He's concentrating on where he wants the ball to go and what his strategy will be once it goes there. He's able to think ahead, to be strategic.

How do you get a subordinate to this level? Only two things promote this transition: practice and reinforcement.

As a leader, you reinforce the employee's efforts not only by your words or monetary incentives, but by being a role model. If you shoot from the hip instead of doing a thorough Situation Review, if you jump to conclusions rather than performing a Cause Analysis, if you push favorite alternatives in lieu of going through the Decision-Making steps, you've got to expect that your subordinates will do likewise.

In addition to being a good role model, you can help your subordinate reach this ultimate stage by making your expectations clear. Employees have an amazing ability to figure out their boss's expectations. If you expect detailed analysis, that's what you'll get. If you expect a rational process rather than an educated guess, you'll get that, too.

Just as you've learned what works and what doesn't with your boss, your subordinates have you pegged. Show them you genuinely care about consistent application of the thinking skills, and you'll see them motivated to follow suit.

Developing the thinking skills in others must be a managed process involving specific behavior by you. As a leader, you needn't be an expert in the learning process. But you must be committed to making the learning process work.

It's important to recognize, though, that there are times when it's best to remain in Conscious Competence, the third stage. For example, I've done a lot of business with some of the world's largest airplane manufacturers. That's an industry in which thinking skills—and especially Plan Analysis—are viewed as tremendously important. Leaders hold problem prevention as sacred as the public hopes they do.

Pilots, for instance, should never fly in the Unconscious Competence mode. So great are the risks, so many and minute are the critical details, that pilots should never slip into "automatic pilot" and become overconfident. Instead, they must force themselves to concentrate on each step of the flight process. Most airplane accidents are caused by pilot error—that is, pilots being over confident and not staying in Level Three.

Again, here are the four stages of learning and what's required to advance to each new level:

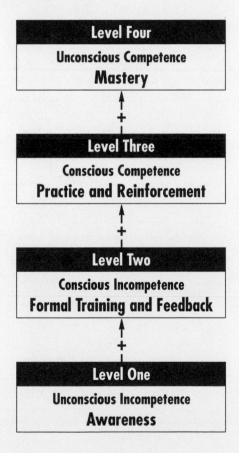

With the explosion of information in the past decade, the need for these skills has increased exponentially—and thus the need to teach new leaders to cope with this avalanche of data. As the organization's batting average improves, more dollars will automatically flow to the bottom line.

Do that and you'll make your mother proud because you'll be ensuring that the cream really does rise to the top.

Chapter **Eight**

How to Solve People Problems Using the Thinking Skills

The pair of events slap you—*one! two!*—almost simultaneously and before you've even had a chance to savor your morning glass of orange juice at your desk at U.S Technica.

First, you see the stiff memo from your boss, Elaine Brown, manager of U.S. Technica's District No. 3. She's a fast-rising star in the regional telecommunications firm who's known for getting quick results—*or else!*

INTEROFFICE MEMO

To:	Repair Supervisor, District 3
From:	Elaine Brown, Manager, District 3
Date:	May 2
Subj:	Unsatisfactory repair trend for April

Results of our April customer-satisfaction survey suggest a major problem with your personnel. Despite the recent transfer of five additional repairpersons into District 3 and the company's heightened emphasis on customer service, customer dissatisfaction *rose*— not declined—last month. Almost all the complaints involved slow response time.

While some other districts posted unsatisfactory ratings ranging from 1.1 percent to 3.2 percent of total responses in April, customer dissatisfaction in District 3 rose from 1.2 percent in March to 6% in April.

Clearly, this is unacceptable and must change immediately. Please plan to meet with me at 9 AM tomorrow to tell what you have done or will do to correct this egregious situation. I shouldn't need to tell you that there can be no higher priority than seeing that all our customers feel courteously and effectively dealt with.

Secondly, as you're reading that over for the fourth time and trying to keep your anger and frustration in check, Jerry Smith, your new assistant, strolls in, agitated.

"Hey, I'm afraid we've got a morale problem," he starts out. "Some of those new repair people who were transferred over from District 2 are still upset. And I've been told that some of them are being rude to customers. I "discussed" this with them this morning, but I'm not sure it sunk in. Maybe it's time you brought in the heavy artillery and really let them know which side their bread is buttered on."

All of a sudden, you've got a major crisis on your hands. You're getting pressure from above and below because of something that isn't your fault and shouldn't be happening. Until recently, your fast-growing district had one of the best customer-service records in the company.

Then, a month ago, an additional five repair personnel were transferred from District 2 to help out with the increased workload. Some of them were said to be none too happy about the move.

The problem seems clear: the new people aren't pulling their weight. They may even be deliberately undercutting the repair department.

The answer seems clear, too: Come down and come down hard on those ungrateful malcontents who ought to be glad they have a job. Make them feel the heat so that, hopefully, they'll see the light.

That should get customer satisfaction and appease Elaine Brown, who's someone you definitely want on your side. It'll also gain the respect of Jerry Smith, who's new to management and looking to you as a role model.

One swift move—and that *should* do it.

Or will it?

It's easy to see the benefits of applying the thinking skills to problem solving in, say, manufacturing. There you're dealing with hardware and tangible products, none of which have feelings, motives, or attitudes.

But can a rational process be applied to people? By nature, people are unpredictable, emotional, and frequently resistant to change.

Still, the answer is yes, you can use a rational process—but with important distinctions.

In a way, the thinking skills are even *more* important in dealing with people than with inanimate objects. The ability to manage emotion and look at the facts objectively is the foundation of all the thinking skills.

People problems, such as the one at U.S. Technica, are often presented in a vague manner ("Hey, I'm afraid we've got a morale problem . . ."). In addition, it's easy to introduce your own feelings into the mix (e.g., fear of incurring the displeasure of the powerful Elaine Brown.)

To guard against these pitfalls, to minimize subjectivity, it's important to ask the right questions before you act. Doing so can be an especially valuable tool in sorting out and resolving problems involving human beings. It can spare you and others a lot of pain and expense later on.

Defining a People Problem

What is a people problem? Think about that. It's not just someone who's different from you or me. It's someone whose *behavior or performance* deviates from what's expected, and the cause of that deviation is unknown.

Does that remind you of anything you've read earlier? Sounds a lot like the definition of a problem in Cause Analysis in Chapter 2, doesn't it? (*"A problem is a deviation from a standard with an unknown cause."*)

Yes, Cause Analysis is the skill that's normally used to bring to bear on people problems. Thus, the kinds of questions we used in Cause Analysis in looking at the Beker-9 situation would parallel the ones we'd use at U.S. Technica.

But, first, it's important to be aware of some concepts that set people problems apart from product problems.

Unpredictable Reactions

When dealing with a machine, you can make a change and expect the same result each time. When dealing with people, the opposite may be true. One change might produce 20 different reactions among a group of 20 people. So learning to anticipate and consider human reaction is an important skill for the proactive leader.

Lack of Quality Data

Human beings don't always say what they mean. They also tend to interpret rather than simply report what they observe. For example, a supervisor may say a worker has "a bad attitude" when the real behavior at issue is the person's tardiness, which might be caused by a medical or psychological problem, a childcare issue, or even something as simple as unreliable transportation. The effective leader must be able to ask the right questions in order to extract fact from interpretation.

Bias and Emotionalism

Our biases and emotions can cause us to see and hear selectively, and that trait can confuse rather than clarify issues. If someone says flatly, for example, "These younger people don't care about the quality of their work," it's clear that a bias has surfaced. Again, precise questioning can be valuable in sorting out fact from beliefs.

Unclear/Unrealistic Expectations

Sometimes what appears to be poor performance is really the result of an expectation not being clearly communicated. So the standard must be clear and understood by the people, and the expectation must be in reasonable proportion to the skills of the person.

Lack of Feedback

Of all the difficulties in managing people, providing feedback—whether positive or negative—may be the most critical.

Often a performance problem happens repeatedly because a person hasn't been told the performance is below par. Providing feedback may be all that's needed to get the performance up to standard. Research has shown repeatedly that people can be motivated by positive feedback and recognition. Again, keeping such feedback objective and "process-oriented" is important.

Back at U.S.Technica, your first instinct is to go to the repair office and knock heads. Read those people the riot act. Jerry Smith will be impressed by your quick response, and you can report tomorrow to Elaine Brown that you've dealt quickly and swiftly with the problem. Then, you'd keep your fingers crossed that the customer-satisfaction figures for May will bear you out.

If the problem *is* unhappy transferees who are deliberately slow in responding to service calls . . . and *if* you can succeed in scaring the living daylights out of them . . . this strategy might work. And you then would likely see better results next month.

But what if the situation is more complex than that? You may have used a hammer when a scapel was called for. And you could end up making the department's problems worse.

So, you think, Maybe I should spend a little time getting a better grip on what exactly the problem is and what might be causing it. You remember your Cause Analysis training. You remember being warned about the dangers of hunches and guesses. You remember the advantages of using a Cause Analysis worksheet.

So instead of running over to the repair shop and making accusations, you grab a People Problem Analysis Worksheet (modified from the basic Cause Analysis worksheet), and go to work.

STEP ONE

State Problem

An accurate, concise statement of the performance deviation gives you a solid base for fixing what's wrong. You come up with this clear, simple statement of the problem: "Repair department has an unacceptably slow response time."

STEP TWO

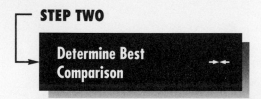

Determine Best
Comparison

Then you will want to use observable facts to describe the specifics of the problem to set up a solid comparison.

You must avoid emotional words or generalizations. For example, Jerry's phrase, "We've got a morale problem," is his feeling, but isn't an easily analyzable fact. Stick to specific statements. And remember: Good questions result in hard facts. So you come up with these questions to define the problem:

WHO?	Who's performing unacceptably?
WHAT?	What undesirable performance is being observed?

WHERE?	Where, geographically, is the poor performance occurring?
WHEN?	When was the undesirable performance first seen? When in the worker's career or job cycle was it first observed? Is it a random, cyclical, or constant pattern?
MAGNITUDE?	How much of the person's performance is unacceptable? Is that unacceptable performance increasing, decreasing, or staying the same?

Next, to really be able to analyze the problem, you need to gather comparative facts so you can compare and contrast, just as we as we did in the Beker-9 Cause Analysis. In the case of U.S. Technica, you're comparing performance before and after April 1, when the decline in performance began.

One of the first things that catches your attention is Jerry Smith's comment that there are rumors that the newly transferred repairpersons were being rude. However, Elaine Brown's memo specifically says "almost all" the complaints were about slow response time.

Rudeness apparently didn't show up as a significant customer complaint on any of Elaine Brown's reports. And usually customers are very quick to complain about that kind of behavior.

That gets you thinking that maybe the rumor mill in this case isn't very accurate. This makes you even more determined to try to keep to the facts and not get carried away by emotions or hearsay.

So you call Elaine Brown's office and request more figures about district operations as a whole. Those statistics show that, while the number of repairpersons in your district increased in April, the number of district clerks did not change. And it's the clerks who relay the customer-service calls to the repair personnel in the field.

Hhhmmm! You wonder: if the repairpersons don't get the requests for service, how can they make the repairs on time?

Similarly, if the repairpersons are delayed, it's the job of the clerk to contact the customer and give a new estimate of when the repairperson can arrive. If the clerks are overloaded, they may not be doing that.

You enter your Comparative Facts on the worksheet, completing Step Two.

Problem Description	**Observed Facts** Identify what you know about the problem as specifically as possible.	**Comparative Facts** Reasonable and logical comparisons: things that are most similar to, but not the same as, the Observed Fact.
Who Who is performing unacceptably?	District 3 repair staff (incl. transferees)	Other district repair staff, or dispatch clerk
What What undesirable performance has been observed?	Slow response time	Inefficient, discourteous
Where Where geographically is the poor performance occurring?	District 3	Other districts
When When was the undesirable performance first seen?	April 1 - 30	Prior to April, back to November
When in the worker's career or job cycle was it first observed?	Customer contacted for RCS	Could have been observed/reported by dispatch clerks at call back
Is it a random, cyclic, or constant pattern?	Random	Cyclic or constant
Magnitude How much of the person's performance is unacceptable?	6% negative customer response (4.8% above acceptable)	1.2% or lower
Is the undesirable performance increasing, decreasing, or staying the same?	Increasing (April vs. March)	Decreasing or stable

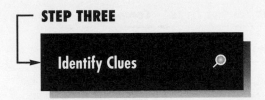

STEP THREE

Identify Clues

Many differences exist among individuals and groups. Physical and psychological distinctions are a fact of life. The key here is to try to concentrate on the work environment rather than make conclusions about people's attitude and motivations. The latter are often useless because they're not facts but interpretations.

So, trying to be objective, you distill some clues from your comparison as follows:

1. Five repairpersons were transferred to District 3 on April 1. This requires longer commutes and thus inconveniences them.

2. The additional repairpersons don't know the District 3 territory as well as the rest of the district repair personnel.

3. The ratio of clerks-to-repairpersons was reduced because no clerks were added to match the new repairpersons.

4. April's weather was much stormier than March's, and this may have slowed response times.

You're pleased with that list. You think you've done a good job of thinking through all the possible differences and changes and then figuring out which ones are really relevant and, thus, can be likely causes of the problem.

Comparative Facts ← Reasonable and logical comparisons: things that are most similar to, but not the same as, the Observed Fact.	*Clues* 🔍	
	Differences	*Changes*
Other district repair staff, or dispatch clerk	5 additional repairpersons transferred on 4/1; number of clerks remains unchanged.	5 repairpersons forced to commute longer distances. 5 transferees less familiar with District 3 territory.
Inefficient, discourteous	A performance observation versus an attitude.	Ratio of clerks to repairpersons decreases.
Other districts	No relevant differences.	No relevant changes.
Prior to April, back to November	Weather worsens.	Weather makes answering repair calls more difficult.

STEP FOUR

Generate Likely Cause and Verify ⋮⋮

Blame is a common response to a people problem. That's because we too often focus on feelings, attitudes, or personality as a way to find the cause (or, pinpoint the fault). Instead, try to look for changes in the environment as keys to cause and always look at people's performance and behavior rather than your beliefs about their attitude.

However, people, unlike machines, don't always react to change immediately or in discernible ways. Some people have the capacity to superficially accept what they see as unpleasant change …then just mutter under their breaths and await an opportunity for revenge.

So in the U.S. Technica case, we can't rule out the possibility that some repairpersons, upset at their transfer, are acting irresponsibly. But, if wrong, that's an explosive accusation.

So we want to be doubly sure that's the case before we confront anyone. Thus, careful attention must be paid to testing all the causes.

As we look at converting the four differences and related changes to possible causes, there's one we can toss out: the weather.

April weather was especially bad, but it was equally bad at the other districts, too, and their response times were much better. So that can't be the cause of the District 3 problem.

Eliminating that, we're left with three clues which could suggest possible causes. They are:

1. Five repairpersons were transferred to District 3 on April 1. This requires longer commutes and thus inconveniences them.

2. The additional repairpersons don't know the District 3 territory as well as the rest of the district repair personnel.

3. The ratio of clerks-to-repairpersons was reduced because no clerks were added to match new repairpersons.

When you're dealing with hardware and you use a "shotgun" approach to fix your problem, you risk time and money. But if you use that same approach with people, changing things haphazardly, you can end up losing the people, too.

Therefore, hard testing against the problem definition is essential. As mentioned, this is especially critical for people problems; there is little margin for error.

So take the time necessary to think about likely causes and how you would verify each of them.

Likely Cause No. 1: *The five transferred repairpersons are deliberately slowing down as a protest.* You could go back and check their response times versus the response times on their other job.

However, that Likely Cause could be entwined with Likely Cause No. 2—*The new repairpersons were slow because they didn't know the territory.*

After all, April was the first month the new repair personnel were operating in District 3. If they had slower-response times, it may have been not because of their attitudes but because of their unfamiliarity with the district's geography.

So looking just at the response times of the transferees wouldn't be conclusive. You've also got to make sure all of the repairpersons are equally familiar with the area.

The third Likely Cause—*The decreased ratio of clerks-to-repairpersons*—can be more readily verified. Add some more clerks and see if response time improves. That can be done independently of the other two Likely Causes.

So your first order of verification will be:

- Arrange for additional clerks to be transferred, at least temporarily, to District 3, and see if that reduces response time in May. That's the simplest theory to test. It's also the one that seems most logical to you to be the Likely Cause.

- If that doesn't solve the problem, it will point to the repairpersons themselves being slow, either out of malice or unfamiliarity. The unfamiliarity can be tested by special instruction in District 3 geography for the transferees.

- If the problem still persists after the geography lesson, then a work slowdown would be the likely cause. And you will need your best leadership skills to deal with a slowdown. Perhaps some of the repairpeople really do not want to work in the new location. You may have decisions to make about how best to deal with that situation. You may have to take some interim action until you can truly eliminate the root cause of the problem.

So, you've outlined three Likely Causes in descending order of likelihood and ascending order of complexity and repercussions.

You feel sure that you've done a thorough job of outlining the options. You feel renewed confidence in your own ability to analyze a complicated situation and then do what's rational instead of what's impulsive and can cause irreparable harm. Similarly, you'll feel confident telling Elaine Brown you've got a good solid plan for solving the problem with minimal upheaval. You'll also feel confident telling Jerry Smith it's too soon to go in with guns blazing.

You're sure the extra time spent dissecting the problem will work to your advantage as well as that of your subordinates and fellow leaders. You can't resist congratulating yourself: *Well Done!*

Okay, But Now What?

A big difference between people problems and problems with objects or processes is that just because we rationally analyze the facts and draw a conclusion doesn't mean that the feelings will disappear.

It's not like changing a battery in a car. The other parts of the car have no memory or feelings about the previous battery. But with people, you've still got to deal with the residue of thoughts and actions. You can't assume the finding the cause will lead to a simple correction.

Your rookie assistant, Jerry, has already had an emotion-filled "discussion"with the repairpersons about their attitude. He may have repeated to others the rumors that repair personnel have been rude, though facts now seem to suggest the problem isn't rudeness and may not directly involve the repair personnel at all.

So even though you think you've done an enviable job of getting to the bottom of the issue and can enlighten both Jerry and Elaine Brown, you've got to deal with the repairpersons. First, they may already be upset at being transferred—and then getting scolded and bad-mouthed, too, hasn't made it better.

You make a mental note to yourself: I'm going to make it a priority to build bridges to the repairpeople, especially the transferees. Otherwise, if they are resentful it could cause other problems down the line.

What Else Can You Do?

As you can see, People Problem Analysis can be a very powerful skill. It can be a big help in avoiding damaging, emotion-filled responses that generally cause other problems. At U.S. Technica, your first reaction not only could have been wrong, it might have poisoned relations with your employees permanently.

But, even so, you have some fence mending to do. You want your employees to feel reasonably content. To do so, they're going to need to feel appreciated and listened to.

Here are five basic principles of people-handling which, when practiced in combination with People Problem Analysis, will go a long way toward helping you to handle people effectively.

The Five Basic Principles

1. Maintain the Self-Esteem of Subordinates

Performance improves as people feel more confident. Good leaders take advantage of that by seizing opportunities to commend their subordinates. Even when it's necessary to discuss a performance problem, good leaders first commend a positive characteristic, then discuss the "improvement opportunity."

In truth, people tend to fulfill the expectations others hold for them. By expecting—and showing you expect—the best from your subordinates, you have a much better chance of getting it. Conversely, destroying the self-esteem of others will guarantee poor performance.

2. Focus on the Problem, Not on the Personality

Because dealing with people problems is often uncomfortable, many leaders have difficulty focusing on specifics. If Jerry Smith had looked into the facts instead of yelling at the repairpeople for reported rudeness, much of the illwill at U.S. Technica might have been avoided.

But when leaders attack a subordinate's attitude or personality, it almost certainly puts people on the defensive, regardless of the facts. It's just human nature to be more threatened by criticism of our attitudes or personalities—which we feel are impossible to change—than by criticism of our performance, which most of us believe can be modified.

3. Use Reinforcement as a Tool to Motivate

Conditioning people to expect a positive response—say, praise or a bonus—when they take desirable actions and to expect a negative response (or no response) to undesirable actions can be a powerful motivator.

Unfortunately, many leaders are more inclined to give negative responses than positive ones.

Take the case of a person who comes late to work, explaining that car trouble made it necessary for him to arrange another ride. The skilled leader would see an opportunity to praise the employee for making the extra effort to come in, even though late. The less skilled leader might merely bawl out the person for being late.

The skilled reinforcer responds as soon as he or she notices the behavior, makes the response clear and direct, and uses extra reinforcement initially to jump-start the correct behavior or discourage incorrect action. Once the desired performance is attained, the frequency of reinforcement may be reduced or directed to another area of performance.

4. Listen Actively

This means satisfying people that they are being heard and that you are open to a discussion. This can be especially valuable in emotional exchanges.

Active listeners will tell an upset person that they *understand* both the content and the feelings the person has expressed even if they don't necessarily agree.

A salesperson, for example, might storm into the production manager's office, complaining,

"You people are incompetent and have never met a deadline. I'm about to lose a key account because your people can't fill an order. What's wrong with them?"

The production manager could best respond by nodding and stating calmly,

"You're concerned about whether we can meet a deadline for a key client. I can understand that. Let's talk about it and see what we can work out."

5. Keep Communicating

It's easy to fall in the habit of giving up on a person who's not performing well. You've told him about the problem, he hasn't responded as well as you'd like, so a wall of disapproving silence falls between you.

But a skillful leader continues to work with the employee, making certain that the goals have been defined and are understood. The leader sets a specific date for review, continues to encourage progress, and sends the signal that he or she has not given up on the person. This will help build the person's self-confidence and motivate him to keep trying to do better.

After the Storm at U.S. Technica

You had your meeting with Elaine Brown, and you convinced her that the situation was a little more complicated than it appeared at first glance, that the repair personnel alone may not be at the root of the problem. You explained your three-step plan for getting at the root cause.

She said she understood and promised to add some clerks to see if that helped. But, she added, she's going to be looking very closely at next month's figures. You got the message. You're proud of how you used the thinking skills and the People Problems Analysis. That allowed you to avoid making a bad situation worse. But what do you do now?

Well, get to work on building those bridges to the repairpersons. Make sure they know, for starters, how important customer satisfaction is in the increasingly competitive world of telecommunications. Explain the possible problem with the clerks and District 3's slide last month. Tell them you think, despite the numbers, they did pretty well in the unusually poor weather.

Make note of the high expectations the district manager has for them in May. Mention that you regret any inference that they've been rude or slacking off and that you don't believe the facts back that up. Tell them you also really want to know if any of them are unhappy with the transfer. Hopefully, as a leader you have created an environment where they can trust you to help them relocate back to their old district if they are not happy in the new one.

Emphasize that you realize the inconvenience the transferees have had to endure, that it was done for the overall well-being and profitability of the company, and that you're committed to making that transition as smooth as possible.

Tell the repair staff that you want their help in returning District 3 to the top of the list in customer satisfaction. And promise them that you're going to work on a bonus system— maybe an extra day off, or a free trip, or something of value—for the team if the customer-service complaints decrease significantly in May.

All those things—from reinforcement to making clear your expectations—can be building blocks of your renewed attention to the repairpersons. Treat them with respect, and you'll likely be surprised at how they perform.

Meanwhile, you think, it's time you and Jerry Smith also had a talk. "Jerry," you begin, "have you studied the thinking skills? You know thinking is like a game of golf. . ."

Index

A

Adaptive action, 44
Advocating (the process of)
  analyzing the decision maker, 119-123, 134
  analyzing the influence network, 126
  creating advocacy tactics, 128-132
  creating an idea profile, 118-119
  creating an influence-network list, 123-125
  defining, 114
  identifying the checkmate decision, 118, 119, 126, 127
  preparing for the advocacy presentation, 133-135
  and the roadblocks to change, 115
  a scenario requiring, 113-114, 116
  steps in, 117, 132
  a tactical strategy for contacting the influence network, 126-128
Alarm, defining the term, 82

B

Brainstorming
  example of, 97-98
  principles of, 95
  about specific solutions, 102
  techniques for, 96

C

Cause analysis, 1, 19, 146
  choices of action in, 44
  decision making versus, 48, 50
  defining, 17

Cause analysis—*Cont.*
  determining the best comparison in, 35-37, 43
  diagnosis in, 34
  an example of comparative problem solving, 23-24
  an example illustrating choices of action, 44-45
  an example of the stair-stepping process in, 31-32, 33-34
  generating and verifying the likely cause in, 39-40
  identifying clues in, 37-38, 43
  the payoff for using, 25-26
  and problems with people, 152, 154, 155
  questions to ask in, 26, 144
  the role of change in, 24
  scenarios requiring, 26-31, 41-42
  stating the problem in, 34-35
  steps in, 25-26
  a work sheet for, 35-36
Causes, definition of the term, 31
Checkmate decision, 118, 119, 126, 127
Concerns
  defining the term, 7
  identifying and listing, 7-9
  separating, 9-12
Corrective action, 44
Creativity. See Innovation
Creativity "sandwich," describing the, 88-90

D

Decision making, 1, 17, 19, 146
  cause analysis versus, 48, 50

Decision making—*Cont.*
 the decision maker in the advocating
  process, 119-123, 134
 decisiveness versus, 49
 desirable criteria in, 54, 55-56, 59, 65
 establishing and separating criteria in, 52-
  56
 factors in risk assessment, 62
 the fundamental principle in comparisons
  for, 57
 generating and comparing alternatives in,
  56-60
 identifying and assessing risks in, 60-65
 a key characteristic of decision criteria, 54
 limit criteria in, 54-55, 58-59, 65
 making the decision in, 65
 one of the most common forms of, 50
 questions to ask in, 48, 144
 scenarios requiring, 47-48, 49-50
 sources of risk information for, 60
 stating the purpose of the decision in, 51-
  52
 steps to effective, 51, 65
Decision style, 126
Desirables
 in decision making, 54, 55-56, 59, 65
 identifying the limits and, in the process
  of innovation, 101, 103-107
Deviation
 negative, 24
 positive, 25
Drucker, P., 87

E

Effects, definition of the term, 31
End users, 124
Experts, 124

F

Feedback
 the importance of, for leaders, 140-141
 providing, in managing people, 153

H

Harvard Business Review, The, 87

I

Idea profile, creating an, 118-119
Ideas, implementing. See Advocating
Influence network
 analyzing the, 126
 creating a list of individuals in the, 123-
  125
 a tactical strategy for contacting the, 126-
  128
Innovation, 1
 assessing the feasibility of solutions, 101
 brainstorming and, 95-98, 102
 calculating the risks for innovative solutions, 102-103
 creating potential solutions, 98-101
 defining, 18, 87, 109
 describing the creativity "sandwich" in,
  88-90
 determining the best alternative in, 108-
  109
 developing design criteria for, 92-94
 evaluating the performance of innovative
  solutions, 101
 generating ideas for, 94-98
 identifying the limits and desirables in
  the process of, 101, 103-107
 the key to, 88
 questions to ask in, 145
 scenarios requiring, 88, 89-90
 stating the objective of the, 91
 steps of, 90
Interim action, 44
"It won't work" syndrome, 89

L

Leaders. See also Thinking skills
 an axiom of leadership, 70
 a common mistake, make, 31
 and damage control, 70-71
 the importance of feedback for, 140-141
 improving the judgment of, 138-139
 and the responsibility to teach, 137-138
 understanding the four-stage learning
  model, 139-147
 why it is necessary for, to review situations, 8
Learning model, the four-stage, 139-147

Alamo Learning Systems

Alamo Learning Systems is an international training, development, and consulting firm well known for the quality of its products and the responsiveness of its service. The company has vast experience in improving the quality of its clients' organizations and operations.

Alamo began business in 1976, when a division of Motorola Corporation asked Guy Hale to design and develop a training and organizational change program to improve problem solving, problem prevention, and decision making skills. Thousands of Motorola employees were trained in Alamo's first "Thinking Skills" program, with impressive results.

With this initial success and unique approach to organization improvement, the reputation Alamo established led to the company's rapid growth into an internationally known and respected management and employee development firm. Today, Alamo works with many of the world's leading corporations, including more than 150 members of the *Fortune 500* teaching them to use *The Thinking Skills.*

With many of the concepts taught in *The Leader's Edge,* Alamo developed *The Fast Track*® ISO/QS 9000 registration program. Alamo guarantees ISO/QS 9000 registration in six months for companies that wish to establish ISO/QS 9000 as the platform for developing a long-term continuous improvement system.

> **Alamo Learning Systems, Inc.**
> **3160 Crow Canyon Road #335**
> **San Ramon, CA 94583**
> **Phone: (510) 277–1818**
> **Fax: (510) 277–1919**
> **Internet: alamols@aol.com**